Loving Gr

# Mr. Lund's Guide to Professional Clamdigging ™

A Quirky Workbook        By Steven Lund

The opinions expressed in this manuscript are solely the opinions of the author and do not represent the opinions or thoughts of the publisher. The author has represented and warranted full ownership and/or legal right to publish all the materials in this book.

Loving Grammar: Mr. Lund's Guide to Professional Clamdigging
All Rights Reserved.
Copyright © 2014 Steven Lund
v5.0 r1.1

Cover Photo © 2014 Steven Lund. All rights reserved - used with permission.

This book may not be reproduced, transmitted, or stored in whole or in part by any means, including graphic, electronic, or mechanical without the express written consent of the publisher except in the case of brief quotations embodied in critical articles and reviews.

Outskirts Press, Inc.
http://www.outskirtspress.com

ISBN: 978-1-4787-2201-4

Library of Congress Control Number: 2013921298

Outskirts Press and the "OP" logo are trademarks belonging to Outskirts Press, Inc.

PRINTED IN THE UNITED STATES OF AMERICA

## DEDICATION

I dedicate this book to the memory of my two best English teachers—first, to my beloved mother, Mae Lund, who first taught me to love language and literature; second, to the legendary Professor Walther G. Prausnitz of Concordia College (Moorhead, MN), who could snarl with the best (all bark and no bite, as far as I could see) and thereby always get the best out of me.

**Steven Lund**

# PREFACE

Several years ago (more than I care to say), when a change of careers brought me to high school teaching, I discovered that I had been assigned to teach a section of 10th Grade Grammar and Writing. One day while doing a lesson on commas, my students and I came upon the following sentence in an exercise book:

(Put commas in the following sentence.)

> Trapped on a sandbar by the incoming tide the amateur clamdiggers Pete and Don who could not swim had to be rescued" (Warriner 535).

Go ahead. Be my guest. Put the commas in.

At the time I had no idea what an "amateur clamdigger" was. I still don't, but the pathetic and dramatic need of the two pivotal characters in this curious sentence—not to mention the desperate and hopeless look on the faces of my students, who were trying to figure out where to put the commas in the sentence—illustrated for me the genuine need of students for some gentler guidance and help.

With this in mind, I set about the task of developing a series of lessons for my students. The goal of these lessons was NOT to introduce my students to all the *chilly* depths and the **thrilling** majesties and the mysteries of English grammar. Rather it was to point a steady spotlight on one problem—**punctuating sentences with commas and semicolons**—and to keep the spotlight and the student's attention there until he had mastered the job. (Note: by the way, I choose the masculine pronoun here since it is well known, I hope, that female students are not nearly as far behind the 8-ball in this respect as male students. My evidence is anecdotal. I am male—I freely admit it, and I'm absolutely positive that my female peers in high school knew more about commas and semicolons than I did.) That is the one principle objective of the book; kindly consult the Contents for the secondary objectives. If students learn something else about grammar from this book, that is their own responsibility and will, I'm sure, lie deeply and heavily on their own consciences and not on mine.

Therefore, it is with delicious and puckish pleasure that I dedicate this tiny book to all Amateur Clamdiggers of the English-speaking world who have longed for simplicity, clarity, order—and an occasional snarl of humor—along the rocky road that leads to the correct punctuation of foreboding sentences like the one cited above. After all, if you can punctuate **that** one, what can't you accomplish in your own lifetime?

**Happy Clamdigging—whether it be Amateur Clamdigging, Semi-pro Clamdigging—or Professional Clamdigging!™**

Dallas 2013

lovinggrammar.com

# EDITOR'S NOTE

Much of the text of this book consists of interactions between the teacher (Mr. Lund) and three fictional students (Felix, Giovanni, and Kristy). This gives the reader—we hope—a sense of actually being there in the classroom and experiencing the inevitable frustrations and despair as well as the happy epiphany moments that all students face in learning a subject as complex as grammar.

Sometimes the dialogue is between the teacher and one of the students. At other times there may be three or even four people talking back and forth. If it is Mr. Lund and one student who are interacting, then Mr. Lund's comments appear furthest to the left and the first student's comments are indented. If a second student joins the conversation, then that student's comments are indented another half inch.

Also, we have used quotations marks throughout when there is specific interaction between Mr. Lund and some of the students. However, when the instructor is putting up "slides" for the students (and the reader)—like **mastery rules** and **memory sentences**, or speaking lecture-style to the class as a whole—we have dispensed with the quotation marks.

Finally, we should note that some readers may see a paradox in the stylistic approach of this book. We are teaching Standard Written English, yes, but the interactions are often light-hearted and informal. Make no mistake: the lessons presented here are straight-ahead, serious grammar, but we have found also that what students often enjoy most about this book is the back and forth camaraderie between the teacher and the students. And yes, there are a few puns and jokes along the way, and yes, we may chase a wild hare or two down a rabbit hole in the next yard, but I assure you: we will get the job done, and we will do it in fine style. And we think the discerning Clamdigger will easily be able to differentiate between the formal and informal styles of writing presented here—both of which, by the way, are essential tools of communication in contemporary culture.

Students who've used the book often speak of sensing that the teacher is somehow right there with them. I think the technical term for that phenomenon is "voice" and that is exactly what we want most of all: to engage the reader deeply in this rather slippery subject that most students consider, on the one hand, too high and mighty or, on the other hand, deadly boring—neither of which lends itself to effective and long-lasting learning. That, in a nut shell, is the essence of teaching Professional Clamdigging™.

Note to the student about memorization:

Your teacher is **duty bound** to hold you accountable for the memorization in this book. This is really the linchpin that will help you to hold this material together and access it in your writing and punctuating life.

In case you're interested, countless students have told me that they **absolutely cannot memorize** a list of words or a rule or a memory sentence. In spite of all these (sometimes histrionic) protests from the students (and even, at times, parents), **I have never found a single student in over 30 years who couldn't do this** when the rubber met the road. As one of my former Clamdiggers put it (and she was one of my best students!), "I did get some zeros because of the memory sentence tests, but now I really know the material."

Happy Clamdigging!

# Contents

**Preface**     v
**Editor's Note**     vii

## Chapter 1: The Noun 'Move' and the Verb 'Move'     1

Lesson 1: Introduction to the Grammar Game     1
Lesson 2: The Four "Moves" of Grammar     10
Lesson 3: Naming the Pieces     17
Lesson 4: Identifying Type I Sentences     26
Lesson 5: Snagging Type II Sentences (and actually understanding DIRECT and INDIRECT OBJECTS for the first time in your life!)     32
Lesson 6: Trouble Ahead: Verbs That Go Both Ways!     40
Lesson 7: Mixing Type I and Type II Sentences     44
Lesson 8: Subject-Verb Agreement: Problem I     52
Lesson 9: Subject-Verb Agreements: Problems II and III     59

## Chapter 2: The Adjective 'Move' and the Adverb 'Move'     73

Lesson 1: Introduction to the Adjective 'Move'     73
Lesson 2: Why the Heck Do We Need Adjectives and Where Do They Go?     84
Lesson 3: The Adverb move     91
Lesson 4: Which is Which? Adjective/Adverb Forms     98
Lesson 5: James Brown Has Arrived with that Answer!     107
Lesson 6: "Good" and "Well"— One Parting Shot     112
Lesson 7: Using Commas with Multiple Adjectives— Coordinate Adjectives Defined     117

## Chapter 3: Punctuating Phrases — 128

    Lesson 1: Getting Started with Phrases — 128
    Lesson 2: Functions of Prepositional Phrases — 135
    Lesson 3: *The Black Hole:* Objective Forms of the Pronoun (me, them, him, her) — 142
    Lesson 4: Participial Phrases: DUM, Da DUM DUM! — 147
    Lesson 5: Generating Past Participial Phrases — 156
    Lesson 6: The Gerund Phrase — 161
    Lesson 7: The Appositive Phrase — 171
    Lesson 8: The Infinitive Phrase — 178
    Lesson 9: Mastery Phrase Exercise — 183

## Chapter 4: Punctuating Clauses — 193

    Lesson 1: Welcome to the World of C L A U S E S! — 193
    Lesson 2: The Adverb Clause Comma Rule and Memory Sentence — 201
    Lesson 3: Busting Sentence Fragments — 206
    Lesson 4: 'Kicking the Tires' of Adjective Clauses — 215
    Lesson 5: 'Who' versus the HATED 'Whom'! — 220
    Lesson 6: Restrictive and Non-Restrictive Adjective Clauses – Here Come the Commas! — 232
    Lesson 7: Lars and the Real Sentence – Commas That Can Change Reality!!! — 239
    Lesson 8: Noun Clauses—"At Your Service!" — 246
    Lesson 9: ATTENTION! Final Review of Clauses — 256
    Lesson 10: Final Review — 258

## Chapter 5: Mickey Mouse, Semi-Colons, and End Game Music — 262

    Lesson 1: Introducers — 262
    Lesson 2: Interrupters — 270
    Lesson 3: More Sick Sentences: Fragments, Run-ons, and Comma Splices — 278

Lesson 4: Who's Afraid of Semi-colons? 291
Lesson 5: The World Famous PROFESSIONAL CLAMDIGGING™ Review—"The End Game" 305

**Appendix** 317
**Acknowledgements** 322
**Bibliography** 323
**Index** 324

CHAPTER 1

# The Noun 'Move' and the Verb 'Move'

## Lesson 1: Introduction to the Grammar Game

"Good morning, my friends. It is my distinct pleasure to welcome you to a strange new adventure called "Professional Clamdigging."

"Hey, wait a minute. What is this? I thought this was an English class!"

"It is. Relax! (I can't even say one thing today without an interruption.) What's your name, anyway?"

"Felix. If it's English, why are you calling it Clamdigging?"

"Well, you sure are full of questions, Felix. That's good; I like that. I like your name too. It's a happy name. Get it? Anyway, if you really want to know, I'll tell you how this course got that name. A few years ago I was teaching a high school English course and one day I called on a student in the front row to punctuate a sentence – Hans was his name; his mother was a college counselor at the school. You want to know what the problem was, Felix?"

"Yeah, I guess."

## CHAPTER 1: THE NOUN 'MOVE' AND THE VERB 'MOVE'

"Okay, as I read the sentence, go ahead and feel free to put all the necessary commas in there in the right places. Here goes:

> "Trapped on a sand bar by the incoming tide the amateur clamdiggers Pete and Don who could not swim had to be rescued"
> (Warriner 1940).

"Now I ask you: is that a sentence or a movie script? In any case, I'll never forget the look on that student's face. I don't know who was in more trouble, Pete and Don or Hans, but I decided right then and there that my students needed to take things a little more slowly. So that's what started it all, my friends, and that's what brings us to our business today: my personal *Guide to Professional Clamdigging.*

"By the way, *Professional Clamdigging* is the highest rank that you can achieve as a writer in my class. And in case you didn't know, **the point of teaching you about grammar is to help you write well.**" (That's the answer to the first review question at the end of this chapter.)

"After all, what is the point of learning chess moves or football or baseball strategy if you don't play the game? Well, writing really **is** playing the game. But before getting up there (where the altitude after all is a bit thin), there are two steps that we need to take first (hopefully without falling flat on our faces). Here are the first two steps:

Step 1: *Amateur Clamdigging* (Chapters 1-2)
Step 2: *Semi-Pro Clamdigging* (Chapters 3-4)


"Oh, good – another question. Yes, Felix?"

> "Two questions. So you're saying that you wrote a whole book just to teach us to put commas in one sentence?"

# LESSON 1: INTRODUCTION TO THE GRAMMAR GAME

"Felix, the journey to Damascus starts with…no, cancel that! I'm not sure you'd ask that question in such a flip way if you knew how complicated that sentence in the box up there really was."

"What do you mean complicated?"

"Well, let me ask you a question. Can anyone in the class give me an example of a non-restrictive adjective clause? Go ahead, write it below."

_____
_____
_____
_____

(A woeful silence ensues.)

"How about a past participial phrase?"

(Hopeless silence.)

"In that case, I think it's time for a brief commercial break. I am offering you my solemn word and testament that by the end of this course, Felix—all of you—will be able to give me sentence examples of these (and all the other structures you need to know to punctuate that sentence or any other sentence in English). Okay, let's go to the second question, Felipe?"

"Felix."

"Oops, sorry, Felix."

"Well, I still want to know why you use 'Professional Clamdigging' for the title of this book."

## CHAPTER 1: THE NOUN 'MOVE' AND THE VERB 'MOVE'

"Okay, Felix. Let me put it to you this way. 'Amateur Clamdiggers' are people who are clueless and stuck, passively waiting for help on sandbars—people like Pete and Don. **Professional Clamdiggers, on the other hand, are confident and competent people who have mastered the subject they are studying.** And believe me, mastering grammar and punctuation is not the easiest thing in the world. But that's where I'm taking you guys, all right, Felix? Would you like to get that kind of confidence in your writing and punctuation?"

"Yeah, sure. I never dreamed I could master this stuff."

"Felix, it will be my pleasure to make a Professional Clamdigger out of you—and everyone in the class. This is like the Marines; no one gets left behind!

And so that brings us to lesson #1. But before I get there, I need to point out to you all that I happen to know that there are some key things about grammar that you don't have a clue about, in spite of the fact you have been studying this stuff since you were knee-high to a Koala bear. Now how in the world am I going to convince you of that? Well, uh, uh…I'll give you **50 bucks** if you can write down a watertight, scientific definition of a sentence."

Write it below:

_____
_____
_____

"That's it? C'mon, get serious. That's the best you can do? You didn't get much sleep last night, did you? This is **50 bucks** we're talking about! Sure, you can use the dictionary. I don't care. It's over there on the file cabinet. Okay, let's hear some answers. Yes, Felix. What's a sentence?"

"A complete thought."

"That's your definition of a sentence, Felix?"

## LESSON 1: INTRODUCTION TO THE GRAMMAR GAME

"Yup."

"Okay. Well I just did it."

"What?"

"I just had a complete thought."

"Where?"

"In my **HEAD**, Felix. As a matter of fact, it was a complete thought about your brilliant definition."

"Very funny, Mr. Lund. It has to have words. **A complete thought in words.**"

"Oops. Now I'm in serious trouble. How's this for a complete thought: '**Never!**' Is that a sentence, Felix?"

"Of course not!"

"Well, it is a 'complete thought.' Check out this little conversation:

> 'When do we get to go on a field trip to the moon, Mr. Lund?'
>
> 'Never!'

"See what I mean? Okay, that's settled. Does anyone else want to try this for $50? What's your name?"

"Giovanni."

"Okay, Giovanni – for 50 bucks, what is the definition of a sentence?"

# CHAPTER 1: THE NOUN 'MOVE' AND THE VERB 'MOVE'

"A sentence has a subject and a verb."

"(Uh oh, now I'm really up against the wall.) Subject and a verb, eh? How about this: **'Baboons like.'**"

"Is that a sentence?"

"No, it needs a uh, predicate."

"A predicate? What the heck is that?"

"It needs something after the verb to complete it."

"Oh, so the subject and verb are not enough, eh? Now we need a predicate. How about this one: **'Planes fly.'**"

"Is that a sentence? It is? So it doesn't need a predicate to complete it. You sure you guys have had grammar before? You sound more confused than Felix, if that's possible. Anyone else? Cat got your tongue?"

"Well, I'm going to take that silence as a sign that I keep my money. Sorry about that."

**I think it's time for the solution. Okay, ready? Here goes:**

Here it is, a **watertight, airtight, scientific** definition of an English sentence. But before I do that, let me explain that I had you guys over a barrel. You see there is not just one kind of sentence: there are TWO kinds of sentences.

**Definition of a Sentence – An English sentence is a group of English words that follows one of two patterns (Type I and Type II).**

Here is the Mastery Rule for finding Type I sentences:

LESSON 1: INTRODUCTION TO THE GRAMMAR GAME

# Professional Clamdigging™ Mastery Rule:

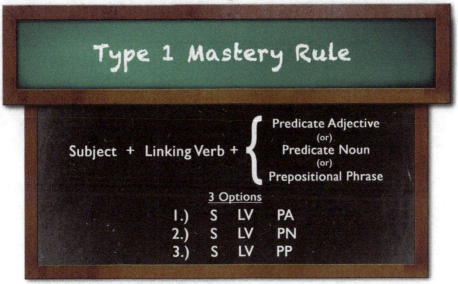

Here are the memory sentences for Type 1 sentences. You will need to write these out from memory for your Chapter 1 mastery test.

## Professional Clamdigging™ Memory Sentence

### Type 1 Memory Sentences

1. Mrs. Lund is brilliant.
      S     LV    PA (describes subject)

2. Mrs. Lund is a property manager.
      S     LV        PN (renames subject)

3. Mrs. Lund is at Thanksgiving Tower.
      S     LV        PP
   (the Prep. Phrase is "at Thanksgiving Tower")

CHAPTER 1: THE NOUN 'MOVE' AND THE VERB 'MOVE'

And here is the mastery rule for finding and identifying Type II sentences:

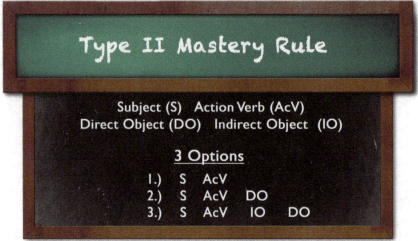

And here are the memory sentences for Type II sentences. Once you have memorized these example sentences, you will be on your way to learning everything you need to do real Professional Clamdigging.

### Type II Memory Sentences

1. Bill lies.
   S   AcV
2. Bill likes Andrea.
   S   AcV    DO
3. Bill gave Andrea a watch.
   S   AcV    IO      DO

(Notice when a sentence has two objects – a direct AND an indirect object – the thing is ALWAYS the direct object and the person is ALWAYS the indirect object.)

## LESSON 1: INTRODUCTION TO THE GRAMMAR GAME

"Got it? Good."

**MASTERY QUIZ ON THIS TOMORROW!** **Warning**: Here's how I'm going to score that quiz (and how I score all mastery quizzes). There are two types of sentences and three options for each. That means six points. But you need to know an example for each option, so now we're up to 12 points. But the biggest problem is that this is a mastery quiz. **That means you'll get either a 12 or a 0**. Nothing in between. **A or F**. So write the information here and make sure you know it like your middle name, so you get a **big fat A** and not the other one.

See you then!

CHAPTER 1: THE NOUN 'MOVE' AND THE VERB 'MOVE'

# Lesson 2: The Four "Moves" of Grammar

Quiz Time!

Okay everybody, take out some paper and we're going to do the mastery quiz that I promised you. I hope you know what you're doing.

**Check your answers with the teacher.**

---

"Let's talk about chess for a minute. Anybody here play chess? Giovanni?"

"I don't see what this has to do with English?"

(Here we go again.) "Don't worry, G-man, it'll all be clear as bottled water in a minute. Do you play chess?"

"Yeah, sometimes."

"Great! How many different kinds of moves are there?"

"Millions probably. My father has a book . . ."

"No, I don't mean that. I mean like forward, backward. How many moves are there?"

"Uh, forward, backward, sideways, diagonal . . . and uh . . ."

"That's good enough for me, Giovanni, my friend. Very good! Okay here's a chart showing you which pieces can make these four moves:

LESSON 2: THE FOUR "MOVES" OF GRAMMAR

## CHESS MOVES

**FORWARD**
Pawn
Rook
King
Queen

**BACKWARD**
Rook
King
Queen

**SIDEWAYS**
Rook
King
Queen

**DIAGONAL**
Pawn*
Bishop
Queen

* only forward (diagonally) one space when attacking another piece

"Notice each chess move can be performed by several chess pieces. For example, a pawn can move forward and also diagonally under certain circumstances, but it cannot move backwards or sideways—ever!

"**This is true also in the game of grammar, my friends.** There are basically **four** important moves or functions in grammar: **the noun move, the verb move, the adjective move, and the adverb move**. Can you handle that? Not 12, not 400, not a million—just four! You will find that different pieces of grammar can do the same move or function as in the case of chess.

"Giovanni, can the queen in chess go straight ahead all the way across the board?"

"Yeah?"

## CHAPTER 1: THE NOUN 'MOVE' AND THE VERB 'MOVE'

"Is there any other piece that can do that?"

    "Yeah, the rook can."

"Right!"

"Now, watch this—you can do the same thing in grammar. It's like magic! Here's an adjective (piece) doing the adjective move."

    Piece: **Adjective**

    Giovanni is the **tall** kid

"The **adjective move** tells *which* kid. So the function is: adjective move. And the piece is: adjective.

"No-brainer, right, Giovanni?"

    "Yeah!"

"Okay, now—watch this."

    Piece: **Prepositional phrase**

    Giovanni is the kid **with red hair.**

"In case you didn't know, 'with red hair' is a prepositional phrase—that's the name of the piece, but it does the exact same function that the adjective did. What's that function, Giovanni?"

    "It tells *which* kid."

"You got it. Way to go, G-man!"

## LESSON 2: THE FOUR "MOVES" OF GRAMMAR

"So here are two different pieces (like the Queen and the Rook) doing the same move. Get it, Felix?"

"Yeah, I think so!"

"Great. Would you like to see one more piece that can do the adjective function? All right, look at this baby!"

Piece: Adjective Clause

Giovanni is the kid **who drove me to school.**

"Isn't that cool? **Which kid?—the kid 'who drove me to school.'**" So three different grammar pieces can do the same move. Everybody with me? You guys still awake?"

"Okay, let's take a look at a chart of the four moves of grammar so you can see which pieces do which moves. (**Warning:** we're going to get into some scary grammar labels and some of you may experience dizziness or shortness of breath as you read ahead.) Remember, my purpose here is not to actually teach you these pieces yet; it is just to introduce you to them—to give you the big picture of where we're going. So, relax and take some deep breaths. You're going to be fine—every one of you. Good luck! Felix, quit shaking the desk with your knee! No one can think with that racket going on."

CHAPTER 1: THE NOUN 'MOVE' AND THE VERB 'MOVE'

## Mr. Lund's Magical Wheel of Function

**1. Noun 'Move'**
Names something or someone

**Nouns/Pronouns
Objects (DO/IO)
Objects of Prepositions
Gerunds
Noun Clauses**

**2. Verb 'Move'**
Links subject to predicate or shows action

**Linking Verbs (LV)
Action Verbs (AcV)
Helping Verbs**
e.g. **Have Gone
Is Talking**

**3. Adjective 'Move'**
Tells more about words that have the noun function

**Adjectives
Adjective Prepositional Phrases
Participial Phrases
Appositive Phrases
Adjecive Clauses**

**4. Adverb 'Move'**
Tells more about words that have the verb, adjective, or adverb function

**Adverbs
Adverb Prepositional Phrases
Adverb Clauses**

## LESSON 2: THE FOUR "MOVES" OF GRAMMAR

"And that's it, folks—all the principle **pieces** and **moves** in the **grammar game.** Are you all okay? That wasn't so bad, was it? Nobody's on the floor. Let me check your pulse, Giovanni. Not bad; you're taking this pretty well, you know that?

"Well, if you weren't sweating profusely before, you are about to get another chance right now because we are about to begin identifying the moves of words. Felix, will you please stop banging your head on the desk? You're going to break it—the desk, I mean. What's the matter?

"No, no, Felix, we're **not** going to diagram sentences. I just need to make sure that you know what key words are in a sentence. You've got to know the chess pieces to play chess, right? Well, the same is true for **grammar**."

**Exercise 1**: Okay, let's see what you guys can do. Identify the function of the words in **bold** below. (Put N for Noun, V for Verb, and Adj for Adjective right after the sentence.) Tomorrow we will make sure that you can all do this in your sleep. Good luck!

1. Mr. Lund's tie looks **funny**.
   _Adj_

2. Clamdigging is not as **hard** as I thought.
   _Adj_

3. Stop banging your head on the **desk**, Felix.
   _N_

4. I did not **run** a stop light.
   _V_

5. I'm really getting **nervous** about this.
   _Adj_

6. Did you **charge** me for those large fries?
   _V_

## CHAPTER 1: THE NOUN 'MOVE' AND THE VERB 'MOVE'

7. You take the **high** road, and I'll take low road.
   _____Adj_____

8. You call that movie **scary**?
   _____Adj_____

9. Where is the nearest **bus stop**, Kelly?
   _____N_____

10. My rich and **difficult** uncle is visiting this weekend.
    _____Adj_____

---

Check your answers with the teacher or go to <u>lovinggrammar.com</u>. That's all for today, folks.

# Lesson 3: Naming the Pieces

"Okay, sports fans—fun and games are over. Now it's time to get down to business. Ready, Felix?"

"What are we doing today, Mr. Lund?"

"Naming pieces is the lesson for the day, my friend. You know the moves of grammar, and now we need to make sure you know the pieces. After all, what's the point of knowing what a Queen does in chess if you can't find her on the board? You're sunk, right? Okay. Can we get started?"

"What kind of pieces do we have to learn?"

"Today we're going to make sure that we can spot nouns and verbs and adjectives, whether in camouflage or not. Now I know what you're thinking: you're thinking, 'C'mon Mr. Lund, I know this stuff backwards and forwards,' and that's swell (and I know that you thought you knew what a sentence was too). The truth is that some of you still don't really know this cold and that's what I want to help you with today. When we're done, everyone in the class—not just Kristy (who has her hand up before I'm even done asking the question)—will know the pieces and you will know them like you know your brother's middle name—ALL RIGHT, ALL RIGHT!—your dog's middle name, then."

**Exercise 2:** Look at the following words and write an abbreviation in front of the word to show if it is a noun (N), a verb (V), or an adjective (ADJ).

1. __V__ breathe
2. __V__ crime
3. __V__ collect
4. __ADJ__ fat
5. __V__ receive
6. __N__ truck
7. __ADJ__ hot

## CHAPTER 1: THE NOUN 'MOVE' AND THE VERB 'MOVE'

"Giovanni, can you please stop the drumming on the desk? What's the matter? You need some help? Okay, let's see. Here are some handy tests that you can apply to each word to see what kind of grammatical piece it is. Would that help?"

"Yeah, I've never gotten the hang of this."

"Well, don't you worry. You're in exactly the right place. This time you're going to get it."

Here are the memory sentences for identifying the main grammar pieces.

### Professional Clamdigging™ Memory Sentences

**Noun Memory Sentence**

(The) _____ look(s) great.
Example: **Sammy** looks great. The **room** looks great.
(**Sammy** and **room** are nouns.)

**Action Verb Memory Sentence**

I, he, she, they (or it) _____ (it) everyday.
Example: I **fix** it everyday. It **breaks** everyday.
(**Fix** and **breaks** are action verbs)

## Adjective Memory Sentence

It (or he or she) is very_____.
Example: It is very **strange**. He is very **tricky**.
(**Strange** and **tricky** are adjectives.)

"Giovanni? Questions?"

"This is fine for people who get it, but I never get it."

"Okay, let's try the tests out. I'll show you how they work. Look at the first word—breathe. What do you think that is? Come to think of it, do it too, Giovanni—very slowly."

"That's easy—it's a verb. I know those."

"Does it work in the verb test? Try it out."

"Yeah, I guess so. '**I breathe every day.**'"

"Right as rain. Good job, Giovanni. Now let's make double sure. Try the word in another test. Try the adjective test."

"Okay: 'It is very breathe.'"

"Sounds pretty absurd, right? '**Breathe**' flunked the adjective test. That means it is not an adjective. A test, if it's a good one, must accept the right words and reject the wrong ones. Whenever a word flunks a function test, make a sound like the basketball buzzer at the end of the game, okay? Can you do that?"

## CHAPTER 1: THE NOUN 'MOVE' AND THE VERB 'MOVE'

"Ngngxxxxxxuhhhhhhh!"

"Louder!"

**"Ngngxxxxxxuhhhhhhh!"**

"Good job, G-man! Now do you see how to do it?"

"Yeah, I think I get the verbs, but the adjectives and the adverbs are the hardest for me."

"We're going to handle the difference between adjectives and adverbs in the next chapter. But for right now let's try the adjective test on all the words on the list I gave you. If a word passes the test, say okay. If it flunks, you know what to do. Here's the list again."

|  | **Mr. Lund** | **Giovanni** |
|---|---|---|
| 1. **breathe** | It is very breathe. | Ngngxxxxhhhh! |
| 2. **crime** | It is very crime. | Ngngxxxxhhhh! |
| 3. **collect** | It is very collect. | Ngngxxxxhhhh! |
| 4. **fat** | It is very fat. | **Okay!** |
| 5. **receive** | It is very receive. | Ngngxxxxhhhh! |
| 6. **truck** | It is very truck. | Ngngxxxxhhhh! |
| 7. **hot** | It is very hot. | **Okay!** |

# LESSON 3: NAMING THE PIECES

"So, which ones are adjectives?"

"'**Fat**' and '**hot**.' I see what you mean. It does work."

"Perfect job, Giovanni. So you have two adjectives. Now everybody figure out what the others are. Write the answers below."

1. *They breathe everyday. verb*
2. *The crime looks great. noun*
3. *They collect it everyday. verb*
4. *It is very fat. Adj*
5. *They recive it everyday. verb*
6. *The truck looks great. noun*
7. *It is very hot. Adj*

---

"Got 'em? What are the answers, Giovanni?"

1. Breathe — verb
2. Crime — noun
3. Collect — verb
4. Fat — adjective
5. Receive — verb
6. Truck — noun
7. Hot — adjective

# CHAPTER 1: THE NOUN 'MOVE' AND THE VERB 'MOVE'

(Dear reader, usually the answers for this and all exercises are provided in the Teacher's Manual, so check with your teacher. Answers and other helpful resources can also be found at lovinggrammar.com.)

"Perfect!! I'm proud of you Giovanni! Yes, Kristy?"

"Can't 'truck' be a verb too?"

"Give me an example."

"They're trucking the strawberries to Maine on Saturday."

"Well, does it work in the verb test?"

"'I 'truck' it every day.' Yeah, it works."

"Okay, then truck can be a noun or a verb."

"Yes, G-man?"

"Maybe it can be an adjective too."

"Would you do the honors, Kristy?"

"'It is very truck.'"

"What do you think, Giovanni?"

"Ngngxxxhhhh!"

"From now on you're my adjective consultant, Giovanni. Yes, Felix?"

## LESSON 3: NAMING THE PIECES

"What's the linking verb test?"

"Getting testy on me, eh? Actually, that's a great question and I'm going to tell you everything you need to know about linking verbs in the next lesson."

**Exercise 3**: Okay, so we know from the function tests that some words can have several functions. Try to find all the grammar functions that the words below can perform (noun, verb, adjective). You three can all work together on this exercise.

1. Light — N, V, Adj

2. Gorgeous — N, Adj

3. Subway — N

4. Sunny — N, Adv, Adj

5. Pledge — N, Adv

6. Cruise — N, Adv, Adj

7. Stupid — Adj

## CHAPTER 1: THE NOUN 'MOVE' AND THE VERB 'MOVE'

8. Stick
   _____N, AcV_____

9. Careful
   _____AcV, Adj_____

10. Dangle
    _____AcV_____

---

Check the answers with your teacher—in fact, buy her a Diet Dr. Pepper while you're at it.

"So it seems that many words can be different kinds of grammar pieces in a sentence. So how do we know which grammar piece the word actually is, Felix?"

"You have to see the word in a sentence to know what it is."

"That's right. Give that man a piece of watermelon!"

**Exercise 4:** Let's take a look at some new sentences. Look at the **bold** words in the following sentences and then put the name of the piece (N, AcV, Adj) in front of the sentence.

_Adj_ 1. Joey's girlfriend is absolutely **gorgeous.**

_N_ 2. We're going to take the **subway** to the concert.

_Adj_ 3. That is not a **stupid** question!

_AcV_ 4. Do you want to **cruise** Greenville tonight?

_Adj_ 5. I wish you'd be a bit more **careful**.

## LESSON 3: NAMING THE PIECES

*N*    6. Please turn the **light** off when you go to bed.

*N*    7. I gave the money to **Sonny** last night.

*Acv*    8. I watched the spider **dangle** on the edge of the window sill.

*Acv*    9. I **pledge** allegiance to the flag.

*Acv*    10. Everybody **stick** your fork in the cake when I count to three.

---

(Check with the boss for the answers.)

"How did it go?

"Do you see how to tell nouns from adjectives and verbs? All right, good. Then we're ready to zero in on the difference between **Type I and Type II sentences**. Then you'll have something to brag to your girlfriend about, Giovanni! You ready? Good! See you tomorrow, buddy."

CHAPTER 1: THE NOUN 'MOVE' AND THE VERB 'MOVE'

# Lesson 4: Identifying Type 1 Sentences

Okay folks, today we are going to roll up our sleeves and get started on **Type I sentences.**

"Hey, hold up there, Mr. Lund. I've got a question."

"Kristy with a question? I thought you did the answers, not the questions. You're starting to remind me of Giovanni, here. All right, fire away."

"Well, I think I heard you say that you would not teach us anything without telling us why we needed to know it."

"Kristy, coming from you, that really makes me feel bad. Or—wait a minute—is it **badly**? Which is it?"

## TIME OUT!

Before we hear Kristy's opinion, **YOU** tell me! Choose the correct one and write it below in the box. Is it correct to say: **I feel bad,** or correct to say: **I feel badly**? And why?

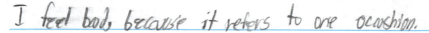
I feel bad, because it refers to one ocashion.

"Okay, Kristy—the envelope, please?"

"I think it's supposed to be bad. **I feel bad**."

"You agree with that, Giovanni?"

"No, I think it should be badly."

"And why is that, may I inquire?"

## LESSON 4: IDENTIFYING TYPE 1 SENTENCES

"I don't know; it sounds right."

"Oh, now that's a watertight reason. And Kristy? What do you say?"

"Mine sounds better."

"Okay, I rest my case. Kristy, **that** is the answer to your question. In chapter 2 we will take up the question of which modifier to use—in this case **adjective** (bad) or **adverb** (badly), and you can't answer that question without considering whether the verb is **Type I** or **Type II**. Okay? Let's learn it first, and then you will put your fabulous new knowledge to work for you in chapter 2."

All right, in our watertight definition of a sentence, we said that there are two kinds of sentences in English: Type I sentences and Type II sentences.

Here are the Type 1 sentences again:

> 1. Mrs. Lund is brilliant.
>      S        LV    PA  (describes subject)
>
> 2. Mrs. Lund is a property manager.
>      S        LV          PN  (renames subject)
>
> 3. Mrs. Lund is at Thanksgiving Tower.
>      S        LV         PP
>           (the Prep. Phrase is "at Thanksgiving Tower")

## CHAPTER 1: THE NOUN 'MOVE' AND THE VERB 'MOVE'

Here are the Type II sentences again:

*Professional Clamdigging™ Memory Sentence*

### Type II Memory Sentences

1. Bill lies.
      S   AcV
2. Bill likes Andrea.
      S   AcV     DO
3. Bill gave Andrea a watch.
      S   AcV    IO      DO

(Notice when a sentence has two objects — a direct AND an indirect object — the thing is ALWAYS the direct object and the person is ALWAYS the indirect object.)

"But wait a minute, Mr. Lund. How do we know when we have a Type I sentence?"

"Very simple, Mr. Felix. **Look at the verb!** If the verb is a Linking Verb, it's a Type I sentence. If the verb is an Action Verb, then it's a Type II sentence."

"Oh, no. Don't tell me we have to memorize a list of words. How many linking verbs are there—600?"

"No way, Felix. Why so sad? Be happy! There are **only 13 linking verbs** that you need to know." (By the way, did you notice that I use a comma before the name of the person that I'm addressing in the sentence, like Felix or Sherlock or Mr. Lund? Good.)

Here they are:

LESSON 4: IDENTIFYING TYPE 1 SENTENCES

# Professional Clamdigging™ Mastery Rule:

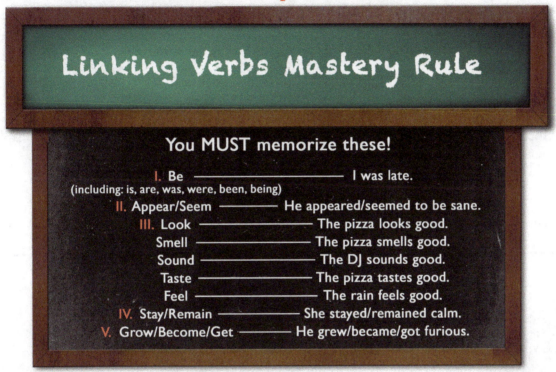

Notice that instead of just giving you a list of 13 random items, I have put the Linking Verbs into five groupings and **YOU MUST MEMORIZE THESE FOR TOMORROW (MASTERY QUIZ)!**

Let me explain these five groups.

# CHAPTER 1: THE NOUN 'MOVE' AND THE VERB 'MOVE'

---

First, you have **be** and all her cousins and relatives—
so we'll think of all those words as one verb group.

Then you have two verbs (**appear and seem**)
that as linking verbs have roughly the same meaning.

The same is true for **stay/remain** and **grow/become/get**.

Group III is the **sense** verbs; in other words, what you experience with your five senses.

Get it?

Okay, let's practice finding these linking verbs.

---

**Exercise 5**: Look at the sentences below and do the following:

1. Find the subject and **underline** it.
2. Find the linking verb and put a **circle** around it.
3. Then find the predicate word and put a **box** around it and above the box put **PA** if the predicate is an adjective (Mrs. Lund is brilliant) and put **PN** if the predicate is a noun (Mrs. Lund is a property manager).

1. <u>He</u> (seems) [confused] *PA* by the assignment.

2. <u>Gina</u> (is) a NASCAR [driver]. *PN*

3. My <u>son</u> (is) a professional [DJ] *PN* downtown.

# LESSON 4: IDENTIFYING TYPE 1 SENTENCES

4. The <u>sky</u> (grew) (black). — PA

5. The <u>firemen</u> (stayed) (calm). — PA

6. The <u>drums</u> (sounded) (pathetic). — PA

7. Your <u>study</u> (smells) (musty). — PA

8. <u>Obama</u> (became) (President) in 2008. — PN

9. Your <u>brother</u> (seems) (friendly). — PA

10. The whole <u>class</u> (remained) (perplexed). — PA

11. <u>I</u> (felt) (sick) to my stomach all morning. — PA

12. That <u>Coke</u> (tastes) (flat). — PA

13. Her <u>health</u> (appears) to be (improved). — PA

14. That <u>barbecue</u> (smells) (divine). — PA

15. <u>You</u> (appear) (satisfied) with that explanation. — PA

16. That <u>hairdo</u> (looks) (bad). — PA

Okay, tomorrow we'll go over the answers, and give you a chance to earn a BIG FAT JUICY "A" or "F" on your mastery quiz. So learn those 13 LINKING VERBS and make yourselves and me as proud as a peacock.

CHAPTER 1: THE NOUN 'MOVE' AND THE VERB 'MOVE'

# Lesson 5: Snagging Type II Sentences (and actually understanding DIRECT and INDIRECT OBJECTS for the first time in your life!)

We're down for Type II sentences today. You know what that means, right? Hey, you know what? You guys are looking kind of anemic today. Are you doing all right? I think it's time for a little **action**! What do you say? No, Giovanni—very funny! No, we're not doing jumping jacks today. I already said—we're studying **Type II sentences** and that means Action Verbs.

"Yes, Kristy?"

"How many are there?"

"Thousands, probably. I don't know. Think of them: **run, jump, spit, crash, cough, smash, love, like** and you name it."

"How many do we have to learn?"

"Oh, I get it; was that your concern, Kristy? Well, here's the **GOOD** news! Ready? No memorization on this one. You know the linking verbs, right? You sure? Write them out—quick!!"

**Exercise 6**: Write out the 13 linking verbs

1. Seems
2. is
3. grew

## LESSON 5: SNAGGING TYPE II SENTENCES

4. _Stayed_
5. _Sounded_
6. _Smells_
7. _became_
8. _remained_
9. _felt_
10. _tastes_
11. _appears_
12. _Satisfied_
13. _looks_

"Okay, then—here's the answer to Kristy's question. She asked if you need to memorize the action verbs. No, you don't because you know the linking verbs, and **ALL** other verbs are action verbs. That was easy, eh? Let me repeat it to be sure that you understand me:

"**If it's not a linking verb, then the verb is an action verb. Got that?"**

Okay, my Clamdigger friends. Now, we're going to go on a hunt for these action verbs. But before we do, I want to identify one structure that you probably have heard about—**the prepositional phrase.**

We will be going into a lot more study of this phrase later in this chapter and even more in chapter 3, but for now, I want to give you a little heads-up about prepositional phrases.

## CHAPTER 1: THE NOUN 'MOVE' AND THE VERB 'MOVE'

When it comes to finding the basic parts of a sentence (how can I say this politely?), prepositional phrases just **get in the way**. Therefore, we will be on the lookout for these pesky little devils, to keep them out of our hair. For the moment, remember that a prepositional phrase is a group of words that begins with a **preposition**. Here are some examples of prepositions: **of, in, on, from, at, about, under, over, between, like**, etc. (Prepositions, by the way, often show the positions of things. You can even see that in the word itself: pre**POSITIONS**. Isn't that cool?)

"Let me show you how this works. Look at this sentence."

>Jenny kissed her brother on the head.

"Anyone see a prepositional phrase here? Kristy?"

>"'On the head.'"

"That's right. So now let's remove that phrase, please."

>"Jenny kissed her brother _____."

Okay, Clamdiggers—I think now we're ready to hunt for subjects and action verbs!

>**Exercise 7:** In the following sentences, **underline** the subject and then put a **circle** around the action verb.

Good luck!

(**HINT**: If you see any **prepositional phrases**—groups of words starting with prepositions like 'over,' 'with,' 'under,' 'in,' 'on,' 'after,' 'like,' 'through,' or 'before,' cross those out so you don't get them confused with the subject and the verb.)

# LESSON 5: SNAGGING TYPE II SENTENCES

1. <u>Korey</u> (hit) a grand slam homer.

2. <u>They</u> (carried) him to the dugout.

3. <u>Rachel</u> (gave) her brother your phone number.

4. The <u>stars</u> (shimmered).

5. Don't (break) that chandelier!
   [<u>You</u>]

6. The lawn <u>mowers</u> just (left).

7. Aunt <u>Kelly</u> (gave) a sweater to me.

8. The <u>hurricane</u> (smashed) into the shoreline.

9. <u>He</u> (stretched) the rubber band.

10. <u>Izumi</u> (played) her violin in the dark.

11. Your <u>sister</u> (returned) the video to the wrong store.

12. All through the night, <u>Marcel</u> (slept) like a bird.

---

Esteemed Clamdiggers, you remember from our first lesson (watertight definition of the sentence) that Type II Sentences can come in three models:

Bill lies.   S AcV

## CHAPTER 1: THE NOUN 'MOVE' AND THE VERB 'MOVE'

Phil likes Andrea.   S AcV DO
(When there is only one object, it is ALWAYS a direct object.)

Jill gave Andrew a watch. S AcV IO DO

Remember, when there are two objects, one is the **direct object** and the other is the **indirect object**. When we have a direct and an indirect object, the direct object is usually a thing (like a watch) and the indirect object is a person (Andrew) or animal (I gave the cat some food).

Now back up to those 12 sentences up there and find those objects, but before you do that, let me first give you a couple of tips to make sure that you know what you are doing.

### Professional Clamdigging Tip

Tips for finding Direct Objects and Indirect Objects

**Step 1. Take** a sentence:   Bart Simpson gave Allie a kiss.

**Step 2. Find** the action verb:   Gave

**Step 3. Ask** — WHO or WHAT gave…?
Bart Simpson gave — that's your subject!

**Step 4. Ask** — Bart Simpson gave WHAT?
A kiss — that's your **direct object.**

**Step 5.** Bart Simpson gave a kiss TO WHOM?
To Allie — that's your indirect object.

# LESSON 5: SNAGGING TYPE II SENTENCES

"Got it? Way to go, Giovanni—you mensch, you!"

Okay, I'm ready to set you all loose on that exercise, and I know that you are panting like greyhounds ready to race.

**Exercise 8:** Now, reread those 12 sentences on page 35, and look for the objects and **fill in the blanks** below. (And—don't forget: any word in a prepositional phrase **cannot be** either an Indirect Object (IO) or a Direct Object (DO). Also, if there is no IO or DO, put a line in the blank.)

|    | IO | DO |
|----|----|----|
| 1. |    | Homer |
| 2. |    | Him |
| 3. | Her brother | Number |
| 4. |    |    |
| 5. |    | Chandelier |
| 6. | Me | Sweater |
| 7. | Me | Sweater |
| 8. |    | Bang |
| 9. |    | Band |
| 10.| Her | Violin |

CHAPTER 1: THE NOUN 'MOVE' AND THE VERB 'MOVE'

|    | IO | DO |
|----|----|----|
| 11. | Stove | Video |
| 12. |  |  |

---

### Professional Clamdigging Tip

"Did you mark 'to me' in #7 as an indirect object? Many students consider this a prepositional phrase (and therefore NOT an object) because it comes after the word 'to.' I know you agree, Felix; I saw that on your paper. Well, let me show you something kind of funny about this word 'to.'"

    A. Aunt Kelly gave a sweater to me.
    B. Aunt Kelly gave me a sweater.

"Do you see any difference in meaning between these two sentences? That's right, Kristy—not a jot of difference. This is the proof that the 'to' in sentence #7 is NOT a preposition but what grammarians call a surface structure object word that we see only when WHAT condition is met? Kristy?

"That's right; when the DO comes before the IO in English we insert the word 'to' before the DO. When the IO comes before the DO, the word 'to' disappears.

LESSON 5: SNAGGING TYPE II SENTENCES

      DO  (to)  IO
      IO          DO

"Okay, Felix. Here is a sentence with a true preposition 'to' for you to compare."

    C.  Aunt Kelly went to the supermarket.

"Okay, Felix baby! Let's see you make **that** 'to' disappear!"

Actually, this is also true with "for." This word can also be used to mark an indirect object before a direct object. Here's an example:

        She bought the Mozart CD **for** me last year.

        She bought me the Mozart CD last year.

SEE WHAT I MEAN? Welcome to the mysterious world of linguistics.

You know, you guys are getting pretty smart—you know that?

See you tamale! And I may have some bad news for you."

CHAPTER 1: THE NOUN 'MOVE' AND THE VERB 'MOVE'

# Lesson 6: Trouble Ahead: Verbs That Go Both Ways!

"How's everyone today? You ready for some serious Clamdigging? What's the matter, Giovanni? Did you lose your puppy?"

"What's the bad news, Mr. Lund? Let's get it over with!"

"Oh, yeah. Okay. I almost forgot. I assure you, it gives me no pleasure whatsoever to tell you that there may be a dirty little secret that you need to know about linking verbs. You remember those guys? Oh yeah? Well, let's just go ahead and make sure of that. Write 'em all out (all 13!) in the space provided below. I'll give you 27 seconds. Ready—go!"

*Seems, is, remained, felt, grew, tastes, stayed, appears, sounded, satisfied, smells, looks, became.*

"Hey, way to go, Felix—you do know them after all. What are you trying to do, pass this class or what? Okay, well…uh…ah….!"

"What's up, Mr. Lund? Cat got your tongue?"

"Well, that's a fine metaphor to come from a guy named Felix. I just hate when I have to backtrack and make it look like I didn't tell you the whole truth about verbs. How many types of verbs did I say there are?"

"Two—linking and action."

All right, Kristy gets the piece of watermelon this time…but…okay, let's do it this way.

## LESSON 6: TROUBLE AHEAD: VERBS THAT GO BOTH WAYS!

Take a look at this sentence:

That chocolate cake tastes so rich.

What kind of verb does it have? Good, Giovanni—**linking verb**. Okay, here we go (they're never going to trust me again).

Now look at this sentence:

She tasted the sushi with fear and trembling.

"Now, what do we have?"

"The verb is 'tasted' and it's an action verb. I already figured that out!"

"You did? Good for you, Signore Braggadocio. Now explain it to everybody else."

"I don't know. You can just tell that it's not a linking verb."

"But how? Anyone else? Kristy?"

"Well, a 'she' can taste, but a 'chocolate cake' can't taste."

Exactly right. Do you all see that? (No, Felix, please no arguments on this one.)

A. That chocolate cake **tastes** so rich. (LV)
B. She **tasted** the sushi with fear and trembling. (AcV)

"So, what are we saying, sports fans? Felix—you get it?"

"I think so. A linking verb can also be an action verb."

"That's it. That's the dirty little secret of linking verbs. So 'tasted' is not equal to 'tasted.'

## CHAPTER 1: THE NOUN 'MOVE' AND THE VERB 'MOVE'

Perfecto. Buen hombre. And why does this matter? Anyone remember why we're learning this? Yes, Kristy?"

"To decide whether to use an **adjective** or an **adverb** to modify it."

"That's right, and if that's not perfectly clear, don't worry. We'll work on that in the next chapter. But remember: the verb in a given sentence is **ONLY** a linking verb **OR** an action verb. It **can't be both** at the same time. So don't go moaning and groaning about how it can be both of them and so you don't know which one it is. That kind of bologna will not fly around here.

"Yes, Giovanni? Why don't I just tell you what it says in Chapter 2? Hey, c'mon, man? Where's your patience? You **lost** it? Great! Well, it's a free country; it's right there in chapter 2—go ahead and read it, see if I care. It's entirely illegal, of course, to read a chapter before it's due, but I guess if you don't tell anyone, no one will know. How's that? Feel better? Are you taking all your vitamins, buddy?" (I'll be quoting James "I feel good" Brown, the soul singer, by the way, in Chapter 2.)

"Okay, let's try to do this MAGIC little exercise (2 different verb functions) with the other linking verbs." (**Hint: it works with all of them except for BE.**)

**Exercise 9**: I'll list the verbs and you **write one sentence using the verb as a <u>linking verb</u>** and then another one **using it as an <u>action verb.</u>** Here we go:

1. Smell   _Acv_ She smelled the flowers.   _Lv_ The tree smells funny.

2. Look   _Acv_ She look at the wall.   _Lv_ It looks very cool.

# LESSON 6: TROUBLE AHEAD: VERBS THAT GO BOTH WAYS!

3. Taste
   He tasted the cake. (AcV)   The taste was so bad. (LV)

4. Feel
   He felt the blanket. (AcV)   It feel like someones watch. (LV)

5. Appear (I'll help you get started with this one.)
   She **appeared** to be late. (LV)
   She first **appeared** on stage at the age of five. (AcV)

6. Grow
   When will he grow up. (AcV)   The tree grew little by little. (LV)

7. Stay
   She stayed there all day. (AcV)   It stayed there all day. (LV)

8. Remain
   I told them to remain here. (AcV)   They remained there all day. (LV)

9. Become
   I ask him to become a dragon. (AcV)   It became a problem later on. (LV)

10. Get
    He was getting on his psy. (AcV)   They just weren't getting the joke. (LV)

CHAPTER 1: THE NOUN 'MOVE' AND THE VERB 'MOVE'

# Lesson 7: Mixing Type I and Type II Sentences

Okey dokey, you now know the only two sentence types in the entire English language like the back of your hand, and it is now time, ladies and gentlemen, to mix them up and see if you know which is which. This is a mastery skill, so make sure that you are alert. If not, see if your instructor will buy you a Coke or something. What? He won't? Nice guy!! Oh well, take a few deep breaths and let's get started.

Here's task number one for today. Below I've mixed together the elements of the two sentence types in English. See if you can sort them out. Please put the two sentence types (3 options in each) next to number I and II. Be sure to use every element.

(IO, PN, S, DO, PP, LV, PA, AcV, S)

I.
  A. _S, Lv LV PA_
  B. _S    Lv    PN_
  C. _S    Lv    PP_

II.
  A. _S    AcV_
  B. _S    AcV    DO_
  C. _S    AcV    IO    DO_

Did you get them? I'll give you the answers in just a minute, so you can check your work. Before I do, let me tell you some reasons why it will help you to remember the parts of these two sentence types.

## LESSON 7: MIXING TYPE I AND TYPE II SENTENCES

Right now, in the beginning of this book, we are just studying the basic functions of sentences:

- Nouns are doing the N function.
- Verbs are doing the V function.

"But if you look back at *Mr. Lund's Magical Wheel of Function* on page 14, you will see that there are some other more complicated pieces that can do the same moves. Look at the Wheel right now and write down for me what pieces in English grammar can do the Adjective function. Felix? Quit stalling. What did you find?"

"Well, there's the adjective and the adjective prepositional phrase and the participial phrase and the appositive phrase and the adjective clause."

"Very good, Mr. Feliz Navidad. Now can you tell me which of these requires commas?"

"No way, I don't even think I know what they are!"

Okay, don't have a cow, man. Let me give you an example:

(Adjective)
1. I saw the **Student Council** President yesterday. (no comma!)

(Adjective clause)
2. I saw the president, **who was shuffling some papers by the window.**
   (comma required)

"Do you know why we need a comma in the second one, Giovanni?"

"No. I thought that was why we were taking this class."

45

## CHAPTER 1: THE NOUN 'MOVE' AND THE VERB 'MOVE'

"Great answer, G-man! And I DON'T expect you to know that until we're done with chapter 3—that will come later. For now just remember that what I'm teaching will really be useful to you very, very soon."

"In a way, it's like football. How many offensive plays are there in football, Felix?"

"I have no idea—hundreds probably."

"That's right. But all those hundreds of plays can be divided into two categories of plays: running plays and passing plays. And KNOWING that a play is a passing play helps you sort out what possible moves the quarterback and the other players will make, right? It's the same in grammar."

"Check the answers on the last exercise with the big boss please, and say hello for me while you're at it."

Look at the following list of sentences. All I want you to do is decide if the sentence is **Type I** or **Type II**. Don't look at me like that, Giovanni! This is not that hard. It's just like if I showed you a film of a football game and asked you to tell me if each play is a running play or a passing play. You can do that, can't you, Giovanni?

"Yeah, I guess."

Okay, just remember (hint, hint!) that if the verb is a **Linking Verb**, it'll be a **Type I sentence**, and if the verb is an **Action Verb**, it'll be a **Type II sentence**.

# LESSON 7: MIXING TYPE I AND TYPE II SENTENCES

**Exercise 10:** Look at the following sentences and decide if each one is a Type I sentence or a Type II sentence. **Put the correct Roman numeral in front of each sentence.**

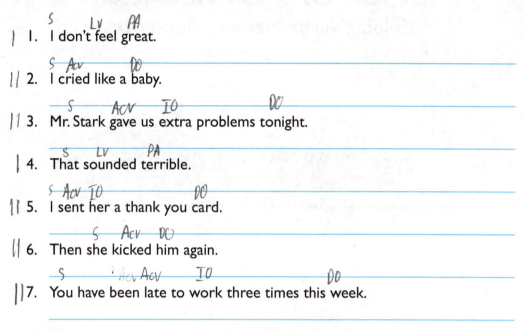

I  1. I don't feel great.

II 2. I cried like a baby.

II 3. Mr. Stark gave us extra problems tonight.

I  4. That sounded terrible.

II 5. I sent her a thank you card.

II 6. Then she kicked him again.

II 7. You have been late to work three times this week.

---

**Exercise 11:** Now, go back and mark the principle parts of these sentences. Find the PA or PN or PP if it is a Type I sentence, and find the objects (DO) and (IO) if it is a Type II sentence.

"While you're waiting to go over the answers, read ahead. There is just one more thing I need to tell you about verbs to help you in analyzing sentences. Both linking verbs and action verbs may have other helping verbs in front of them. Have you heard of helping verbs, Kristy?"

"Sure."

"Can you give us a couple of examples?"

CHAPTER 1: THE NOUN 'MOVE' AND THE VERB 'MOVE'

# Professional Clamdigging™ Memory Sentence

## Helping Verbs Memory Sentences

Kristy's Helping Verb Examples:

1. They **are** running.
2. He **is** being stubborn.
3. You **must have** given me the card.
4. They **didn't** get the package until Friday.

### Professional Clamdigging Tip

Notice a complete verb can have two or three parts. The main thing to remember is that when you are trying to decide what kind of verb you have in a sentence (linking or action), just look at the LAST part or word in the complete verb. This is called the main verb. Let's try this out.

"What are the main verbs in the sentences in Kristy's Helping Verbs above? Felix? Do you have a question?"

"This kind of stuff really makes me nervous. Can we do these together?"

# LESSON 7: MIXING TYPE I AND TYPE II SENTENCES

"Sure, Felix. Giovanni, what's the main verb in the first one above?"

"Is it 'running'?"

"That's right! And what kind of verb is that, Linking or Action?"

"Action."

"Great! So we have a Type II sentence, right? Write down a II next to that sentence please."

"Is the next one stubborn?"

"Kristy?"

"No, stubborn is not a verb. It doesn't pass the verb test. 'We stubborned yesterday.'"

"Good. So, try again, G-man."

"Now I get it. '**Being**' is the main verb in the second sentence and that is a **linking verb** so it is a **Type I sentence**."

"Good job! Kristy, can you do the others?"

"Yeah, 'given' is the main verb in #3 and it is an **action verb**, so that is a **Type II sentence**. And 'get' is the main verb in #4 and that is an **action verb** in this case, so that is a **Type II sentence**."

Here is a more complete list of helping verbs. You don't have to memorize these, but be sure that they do not get in the way of your finding the main verb.

CHAPTER 1: THE NOUN 'MOVE' AND THE VERB 'MOVE'

---

### HELPING VERBS

**1. BE**
(all forms, except **been** which is always a main verb)

**2. HAVE, HAS, HAD**

**3. DO, DOES, DID**

**4. MODAL VERBS:**
**may, might, can, could, will, would, should**

---

Okay, let's do an exercise that puts it all together now.

**Exercise 12:** Look at the following sentences and do the following:

1. Put a **box** around the complete verb.
2. **Draw an arrow** pointing to the last word of the complete verb. ("And, yes Felix: if there is only one word in the verb, then THAT is the last word—the main verb.")
3. **Put LV or AcV** above the main verb.
4. Now based on the type of verb you have identified, **put I or II in front of the sentence** to show which type it is.

(Remember to cross out any prepositional phrases that you see. For now they are just "in the way.")

II 1. We [took] the photos in for processing yesterday.  *(AcV)*

# LESSON 7: MIXING TYPE I AND TYPE II SENTENCES

2. Did you bring the balloons too?

3. I might have been there late.

4. Could you speak louder?

5. The football coach is very upset with us.

6. Brad gave me a call last night.

7. I could be there by 8:00.

8. I haven't seen my favorite aunt in six months.

9. It's getting colder at night.

10. I feel bad about breaking the china.

---

Check your answers with your teacher.

That's it for now. See you tomorrow, Clamdiggers!

CHAPTER 1: THE NOUN 'MOVE' AND THE VERB 'MOVE'

# Lesson 8: Subject-Verb Agreement: Problem I

"Are you guys ready for action? Uh, I'll take that silence for a YES. One thing we now know is the two basic patterns of a sentence, so we are now ready to tackle our first mastery grammar problem—Subject-verb agreement. And the good news, my friends, is that you know more about this than you may think. Watch this: Giovanni's going to prove my point.

"Okay, Mr. Giovanni, here's what I want you to do. Look at the following three sentences and put a C in front of any sentences with correct agreement and put a * in front of any sentence with faulty agreement."

1. John likes Marie.
2. John and Marie loves to play tennis. (hahahahahaha!)
3. We goes to the park every Sunday. (hahahahahahaha!)

"Very good, G-man! #1 is correct and unless your name is Rocky or Rambo or Tarzan, I'm sure you realize that 2 and 3 are not. I told you that you know a lot about this. Now go back and fix those other verbs (#2 and 3) to make sure they agree with the subjects."

"Good man! The correct subject-verb agreement should be as follows:

1. John likes Marie. (singular)
2. John and Marie love to play tennis. (plural)
3. We go to the park every Sunday. (plural)

"Okay, here's the rule. This one's not too tough."

LESSON 8: SUBJECT-VERB AGREEMENT: PROBLEM 1

# Professional Clamdigging™ Mastery Rule:

## Subject – Verb agreement Mastery Rule

When the subject is singular, the verb must be singular; when the subject is plural, the verb must be plural.

Notice that the 's' on a regular verb shows that it is singular and agrees with a singular verb. This is rather confusing for international students: 's' on a noun usually shows that it is plural [e.g. chair (singular); chairs (plural)]. So keep your wits about you—whether you are a native speaker of English or not."

"C'mon, Mr. Lund; let's move this along. This is way too easy."

"Glad to hear that, Felix. Here you go. You do the next one."

The price on the two blue shirts (is/are) too high.

"That's easy. It's 'are' because the subject is plural."

"Whoa. Now, just hold your horses a minute, pardner. Did you say the subject was plural?"

# CHAPTER 1: THE NOUN 'MOVE' AND THE VERB 'MOVE'

"Yeah. Two shirts. That's plural."

"Do you agree, Kristy?"

"No, sir. 'Two shirts' is not the subject—because that is part of the prepositional phrase 'on the two shirts.' We learned that any words that are part of a prepositional phrase cannot be the subject of the sentence."

"Look, Felix baby—let me help you here: cross out the prepositional phrase in that sentence."

The price **on the two blue shirts** (is/are) too high.

"Okay, NOW tell me what is the subject of the sentence?"

"'Price.' Now I get it. 'Price' is singular, so the verb should be 'is.'"

"That's the stuff!! Way to go, Mr. Happy-man!"

Okay, let's back up here and review for a second. Remember in Lesson 5 when we were analyzing sentences with action verbs, we learned that a prepositional phrase is a group of words that begins with a preposition. Here are some examples of prepositions: **of, in, on, from, to, through, into, at, about, under, over, between, like,** etc. Remember, we said that prepositions often (but not always!) show the positions of things, and that we can even see that in the word itself: prePOSITIONS.

To make sure that you have the right subject-verb agreement, get rid of the prepositional phrase and then say the subject and the verb together, and I bet ten bucks you will never make a mistake again, Felix.

## LESSON 8: SUBJECT-VERB AGREEMENT: PROBLEM 1

"Uh, I heard that, Felix, and it wasn't funny. You would actually make an intentional error just to deprive me of ten hard earned dollars? Have you no integrity, sir?"

So look, Clamdiggers—the Professional Clamdigging hint is this:

### Professional Clamdigging Tip

When trying to check subject-verb agreement, always eliminate all prepositional phrases **between the subject and the verb.**

**Exercise 13**: Look at the following sentences. First, see if there's a prepositional phrase in front of the verb. If so, **cross it out**; then **underline the subject**. Finally, **SAY** the subject to yourself (out loud), and then you'll be ready to choose the correct verb form. Ready? Here we go!

1. The leaves ~~on the side of the building~~ (**look**/looks) burned.

2. The plates ~~of meat on the two front tables~~ (was/**were**) just delivered.

3. Her command ~~of foreign languages~~ (**is**/are) astonishing.

4. One Texan ~~in five~~ (**is**/are) in significant debt.

5. The mental health needs ~~of my brother~~ (**demand**/demands) immediate attention.

6. The cause ~~of many divorces~~ (**is**/are) communication breakdown.

7. The secret ~~of her entrepreneurial successes~~ (**was**/were) business contacts.

## CHAPTER 1: THE NOUN 'MOVE' AND THE VERB 'MOVE'

8. The <u>lady</u> from Housekeepers Inc. (want/(wants)) you to call.

9. The <u>purpose</u> of their many contributions ((is)/are) to save us time in the long run.

10. The <u>numbers</u> on the list ((don't)/doesn't) add up.

11. The <u>books</u> in the back bookshelf ((need)/needs) to be dusted.

12. The <u>presence</u> of my family members ((is)/are) always a joy to me.

Check your answers with the boss, please!

---

"Okay, we have just one more issue to deal with before we consider this lesson history. Here's the deal. Kristy, look at this sentence and tell me which verb goes with the subject."

Mr. Lund, in addition to his brother and his three sisters, (has/have) blue eyes.

"Is that true about the blue eyes?"

"First answer the question, and then we'll talk about the eyes, okay?"

"Okay, the subject 'Mr. Lund' is singular, so the verb is 'has'.

"Wait a minute. That's not right! It should be 'have.'"

"No, that's wrong, Giovanni. This is a trick: 'his brother and his three sisters' is part of the prepositional phrase."

"Very good, Kristy. Once again, go back to the grammar hint—cross out prepositional phrases between the subject and the verb. Go ahead, Giovanni."

### LESSON 8: SUBJECT-VERB AGREEMENT: PROBLEM I

Mr. Lund, ~~in addition to his brother and his three sisters,~~ (has/have) blue eyes.

"That solves it, right, Giovanni?"

"Yeah, it does."

"So what about the eyes, Mr. Lund?"

"I'm Norwegian and Swedish in blood though American by birth. Blue eyes are dominant in that class of humans, so yes, I did actually grow up in a ghetto of blue eyes. I think we were the only seven in the city of Chicago. Can we please get back to business now?"

**Exercise 14: Choose the correct verb form** and don't forget to **obliterate any prepositional phrases** between the subject and the verb.

1. John, ~~as well as my cousin Rick,~~ ((is)/are) going to the Elvis concert.

2. Mr. Zimmerman, a~~long with his Advanced Physics class,~~ ((is)/are) performing in the National Kazoo Symphony.

3. Jody and Kim, ~~as well as their oldest son,~~ (is/(are)) coming mountain-climbing with us in Kansas.

4. Tandy, ~~as well as her grandparents,~~ ((has)/have) invited us to dinner at Ganoogle's Pickle Shoppe.

5. Mr. Fry, a~~long with his hunting buddies in Minnesota,~~ (love/(loves)) to sponsor the annual "Save the old growth trees" tailgate party in Tofino.

6. My college roommate, a~~long with his Boy Scout jamboree,~~ ((is)/are) camping in the Scratch Eye, Texas this summer.

## CHAPTER 1: THE NOUN 'MOVE' AND THE VERB 'MOVE'

7. My oldest son, ~~Marcel, and his wife, Izumi,~~ (is/are) visiting Toyama, Japan.

**Check answers with the big bad boss!**

"That's it for today. Don't do anything Kristy wouldn't do, Giovanni. Okay?"

# Lesson 9: Subject-Verb Agreements: Problems II and III

"How much more of this subject-verb agreement is there, Mr. Lund? I want to get to the James Brown!"

"Well, Mr. Felix, the only thing standing between you and the 'King of Soul Music' is this last lesson, which is not exactly a breeze, if you know what I mean. Fasten your seatbelts, everybody, because we've got a bumpy road ahead."

Here's the list of troublesome words, and you are going to have to (how shall I say this delicately) **MEMORIZE THEM**!

## Professional Clamdigging™ Mastery Rule:

### "Strange but Singular" Mastery Rule

"Strange but Singular" Pronouns always take a singular form of the verb.

CHAPTER 1: THE NOUN 'MOVE' AND THE VERB 'MOVE'

# *Professional Clamdigging*™ *Memory Sentence*

## "Strange but Singular" Pronoun Memory Sentence

**Neither** of the **students** seems happy.

---

**Strange but Singular Pronouns**

1. **Each** of the students
2. **One** of the students
3. **Either** of the students
4. **Neither** of the students
5. **Everyone**
6. **Everybody**
7. **Anyone**
8. **Anybody**
9. **Someone**
10. **Somebody**
11. **No one**
12. **Nobody**

⟩ (seem/seems) happy.

---

Okay, now everyone look at those Strange but Singular pronouns. Now, tell me which verb we choose for each one.

"This is a trick, Mr. Lund, isn't it? They're all the same—**seems** happy."

"Well, you sure don't seem happy, Kristy. Why do you say it's a trick?"

## LESSON 9: SUBJECT-VERB AGREEMENTS: PROBLEMS II AND III

"Because you called them all **singular pronouns** and if they're **singular pronouns**, then they should always have a **singular verb** like 'seems.'"

"Well, you may not be happy, but you are correct, Ms. Kristy."

"Okay, Mr. Lund, we've got it. Let's get to chapter 2."

"Yeah okay sure, Giovanni. Just answer this for me. Which is it?"

Either Marcel or Chris **(is/are)** going to pick you up from the game.

"That's easy. It's 'are.'"

"I can't believe you fell right into his trap! No, it's 'is' because he just told you that it was **singular**."

"Well that's not the way anyone talks, Kristy. My mother says, 'Either your brother or your sister are picking you up.'"

"Ahem, no one's correcting how anyone talks, Giovanni—least of all mothers! (For Pete's sake!) What we're studying in this course is how to write in standard English. But if you think about it logically, '**either**' means X *or* Y—in other words one—not both, right?"

"Yeah."

"Okay, so the point is that it's **singular**."

"How about the word 'everyone' or 'everybody'? Why are those **singular**?"

"I guess you have to think of everybody as meaning not the whole group but *ev-ery si-ngle in-di-vi-dual per-son* in the room. Look, think of it any way you want, but that's the rule. Those darned Strange but Singular Pronouns are always singular. Tomorrow we will have a DO or DIE Mastery Quiz on those 12 pronouns."

# CHAPTER 1: THE NOUN 'MOVE' AND THE VERB 'MOVE'

Okay, here's an exercise for us to see if you guys are picking this up.

> **Exercise 15: Cross out any prepositions** you see between the subject and verb, and **circle the correct verb choice**. If you see a Strange but Singular pronoun in the sentence below, be sure that the verb is in the singular form.

1. Each of us (**makes**/make) some errors when we're speaking.

2. One of my sisters (**plays**/play) the harp.

3. Neither of the responses (**is**/are) correct.

4. Either Kelly or Connie (**is**/are) bowling for dollars tonight.

5. Either of those pants (match/**matches**) the jacket.

6. Every one of my friends (speak/**speaks**) pig Latin.

7. (**Is**/are) anybody feeling confused?

8. (**Does**/do) anyone want to get a candy bar?

9. (**Does**/do) any of you actually like English grammar?

10. (**Is**/are) anyone here hungry?

11. One of these verbs (**is**/are) correct.

12. Neither Pat nor Kay (**is**/are) coming to the party.

# LESSON 9: SUBJECT-VERB AGREEMENTS: PROBLEMS II AND III

13. Someone ~~in the back of the room~~ with blue hair (**is**/are) talking too much.

14. Each of us (**needs**/need) to do some soul searching about this.

15. Nobody (**is**/are) to blame.

16. Some people (is/**are**) always ready for action.

**Check out the answers with the teacher!**

---

One more little item (Problem 3) is now all that separates you from the James Brown chapter (i.e. Chapter 2).

This one should not be quite as hard. The words in the box below are known as Collective Nouns, and as the name suggests, when we see a collective noun, we think of the noun as being a <u>single unit</u> or <u>package</u>.

---

### COLLECTIVE NOUNS

| | |
|---|---|
| Team | Squad |
| Group | Committee |
| Jury | Panel |
| School | Government |
| Company | Flock |

CHAPTER 1: THE NOUN 'MOVE' AND THE VERB 'MOVE'

# Professional Clamdigging™ Mastery Rule:

> ## The Collective Noun Mastery Rule
>
> Collective Nouns always go with the singular form of the verb.

For instance, your football coach should say (I don't know if he does):

## *Professional Clamdigging™ Memory Sentence*
### Collective Noun Memory Sentence

> The team **is** meeting for game analysis
> in the locker room right after school.

**Exercise 16**: Okay, this time instead of my giving you sentences, let's do it the other way around. This time you **write sentences for me using the Collective Nouns** in the box above. Use the Collective Nouns in the subject position and be sure that your verb is SINGULAR.

**LESSON 9: SUBJECT-VERB AGREEMENTS: PROBLEMS II AND III**

1. The team won their game.
2. The group ate pizza.
3. The jury drank coffie.
4. The school had a drill
5. That Company sells books.
6. The squad is training.
7. The committee makes decisions.
8. The panel votes on things.
9. The government is hiding aliens.
10. A flock of brids is flying over us.

---

Now, see if you can think of any other words that might go on this list. Put them in the box below.

☐

CHAPTER 1: THE NOUN 'MOVE' AND THE VERB 'MOVE'

**Just kidding! Try this box.**

---

Tride.        Faculty

Troop

---

Before our review quiz, I do need to tell you one more thing. Do you remember in Lesson 7 when I showed you how a complete verb could consist of two or three words like 'is going' or 'doesn't think' or 'hasn't been writing'? Actually, Kristy gave us some great examples of this. At that time I told you to concentrate on the LAST word of the verb phrase to see what kind of verb you have (Action Verb or Linking Verb), right? Let's take another look at those sentences.

## Professional Clamdigging™ Memory Sentence
### Helping Verbs Memory Sentences

Kristy's Helping Verb Examples:

1. They **are** running.
2. He **is** being stubborn.
3. You **must have** given me the card.
4. They **didn't** get the package until Friday.

# LESSON 9: SUBJECT-VERB AGREEMENTS: PROBLEMS II AND III

Well, I hope you can see that now when we are trying to be sure we have the right **subject-verb agreement** that we need to look at the **first** word in the verb phrase. Let's practice this a little.

**Exercise 17:** Look at the verb phrases in the box above and tell me **which is the first word in the verb phrase** that we will use in subject-verb agreement.

1. are
2. is
3. must
4. didn't

**Exercise 18:** Now <u>underline</u> the first word in the verb phrase in the following sentences:

1. Jan <u>will</u> be getting to the airport about 10:00.

2. <u>Are</u> you taking that political science course this term?

3. <u>Do</u> you see Mr. Couser's car in the parking lot?

4. <u>Has</u> everyone turned in the second draft of his essay?

5. <u>Did</u> you hear that rattling sound in the grass?

6. <u>Guess</u> which team is in first place in the AL West Division.

## CHAPTER 1: THE NOUN 'MOVE' AND THE VERB 'MOVE'

7. <u>Can</u> you help me with these problems?

8. It <u>must</u> have rained last night.

9. I <u>would</u> never drive that road during rush hour.

10. <u>Have</u> you heard about the tornado in Oklahoma?

11. Yeah, he really <u>is</u> being a jerk.

---

**Exercise 19:** Put a "C" in front of the sentence if it is correct. If it's wrong, cross out the wrong part and put the correct verb form above it.

1. Laura, as well as Bob, ~~have~~ *has* seen the new Bill Murray movie.

2. The gaggle of geese ~~are~~ *is* heading back north to Canada.

3. Either Ms. Meyer or Coach Krause ~~are~~ *is* in charge of lunch today.

4. Mr. Allmon's friend Sam, as well as his relatives from Illinois, ~~are~~ *is* coming to the auction on Saturday.

C 5. Neither of the middle school basketball teams is playing this afternoon.

6. The cheerleading squad ~~are~~ *is* fed up with the lack of school spirit.

7. Mr. Krause, as well as Mrs. Krause, ~~are~~ *is* doing a dress-code check today.

8. Every one of the office helpers ~~get~~ *gets* the announcements.

# LESSON 9: SUBJECT-VERB AGREEMENTS: PROBLEMS II AND III

9. Each of us ~~plan~~ to attend the prom planning committee.
   *plans*

10. The jury ~~were~~ unable to come to agreement.
    *was*

11. Neither of them ~~are~~ likely to come to the practice.
    *is*

12. His experience with jazz groups ~~qualify~~ him to lead the marching band.
    *qualifies*

13. The purpose of these exercises ~~are~~ to help you write with clarity.
    *is*

14. The principal, as well as the assistant principal, ~~are~~ waiting for you on the phone.
    *is*

C 15. Are either of the art teachers planning to help with stage decorations?

Now, remember the Mastery Quiz tomorrow on:
   1. **Strange but Singular** Pronouns and
   2. Collective Nouns.

### Exercise 20: Chapter 1 Review

1. What is the watertight definition of an English sentence? (Be sure to include the three options of Type 1 sentences and examples of each of those, and the three options of Type 2 sentences and the examples of those also.)

```
  S      LV   PA                    S    AcV
Ms. Lund is Brilliant            Bill lies

  S      LV      ti   PN             S     AcV    DO
Ms. Lund is a Property Monger    Bill likes Andrew.

  S      LV                          S    AcV   IO      DO
Ms. Lund is at Thanksgiving Tower. Bill gave Andrew a watch
```

69

# CHAPTER 1: THE NOUN 'MOVE' AND THE VERB 'MOVE'

2. What are the four "moves" of English grammar?

   Name something or someone
   Linking subject to predicate or shows action
   Tells more about words that have the noun function
   Tells more about words that have the verb, adjective, or adverb function

3. Identify the **grammatical function** of the underlined words in the following sentences:

   Adj a. I love your <u>fabulous</u> new car.
   N b. Are you going to take the <u>subway</u> to the hockey game?
   V c. Did you <u>take</u> anyone to the party last week?
   V d. I <u>gave</u> your lunch money to your brother.
   Adj e. Did you hear about that <u>accident</u> this morning?
   V f. I cannot <u>give</u> you any more money right now.
   Adj g. Are you sure you want to buy those <u>expensive</u> shoes?

4. What is the Noun Test?
   (The) ___ Look(s) great

5. What is the Action Verb Test?
   I, he, she, they (or it) ___ (it) everyday

6. What is the Adjective Test?
   It (or he or she) is very ___

7. Give an example of a word that can have two different grammar functions (noun, verb, adjective).
   Sunny

8. How do you know if you have a Type 1 or a Type 2 sentence?
   Type 1 has linking verbs and Type 2 has Action verbs

## LESSON 9: SUBJECT-VERB AGREEMENTS: PROBLEMS II AND III

9. Write out five action verbs.
   run, hide, talked, gave, took

10. Mark the object in the following sentences as either Direct Objects (DO) or Indirect Objects (IO):
    a. The policeman gave <u>me</u> a ticket for illegal parking. — IO
    b. My boss gave everyone a <u>raise</u>. — DO
    c. Miss Meyer gave me a great Mozart <u>CD</u>. — DO
    d. Kristy saw her <u>brother</u> in the gym. — IO
    e. My aunt gave Tanya a new <u>hairdryer</u>. — DO

11. Based on the Professional Clamdigging Tip in this chapter, which of the sentences below contains the preposition 'to'?
    a. Aunt Kelly gave a sweater to me.
    (b.) Aunt Kelly went to the supermarket.

12. Give an example of the following words as a linking verb and then also as an action verb.
    a. look — She look at the wall. (Acv)  It looks very cool. (LV)
    b. feel — He felt the blanket. (Acv)  It feels like a watch. (LV)
    c. grow — The plant grew last night. (Acv)  When will they grow up. (LV)
    d. remain — They remained there all day. (Acv)  We found the remains of a city. (LV)

13. Mark the helping verbs (HV) and the main verbs (MV) in the following sentences. Write the correct abbreviation above the word.
    a. <u>Have</u> (HV) you <u>been</u> (MV) to Brazil?
    b. <u>Did</u> (HV) you <u>finish</u> (MV) the adjective exercises?
    c. I <u>should</u> (HV) <u>have</u> (HV) <u>helped</u> (MV) him yesterday.
    d. <u>Did</u> (HV) you <u>get</u> (MV) the tickets for tonight?

## CHAPTER 1: THE NOUN 'MOVE' AND THE VERB 'MOVE'

14. When you have helping verbs in a sentence (verb phrase), which part of the verb phrase do you look at to determine if the sentences are Type 1 or Type 2?
    _The Main verb_

15. Which part of the verb phrase do you look at to solve the problem of subject-verb agreement?
    _The subject_

16. Choose the correct verb that agrees with the subject in the following sentences:
    a. Tandy, along with her two cousins, (**is**/are) inviting us to a party at their house.
    b. Either Marcel or Chris (**is**/are) free to help you with the move.
    c. One of the two guys in our class (**is**/are) staying to clean up after the meeting.
    d. The whole football team (**has**/have) agreed to an extra practice on Saturday.
    e. The price of the shoes (**is**/are) too much.
    f. Neither of my friend (**wants**/want) to go to the concert.
    g. One of the policemen (**is**/are) willing to help.

CHAPTER 2

# The Adjective 'Move' and the Adverb 'Move'

## Lesson 1: Introduction to the Adjective 'Move'

"Okay, ladies and gentleman, it's time for a review before we set out on our next venture. Let's review our four grammar 'moves.'"

"Yes, Felix, you can look at your *Magical Wheel of Function*."

"Giovanni? What page is it on? Let me see if I've got this straight, my friend. You don't know what page the *Magical Wheel of Function* is on, and you want ME to tell you where it is? Is that right?????? Okay. It's on page 14!"

Here we go:

1. What is the **noun 'move'**?
   *Names something or someone*

2. What is the **verb 'move'**?
   *Links subject to predicate or show action*

## CHAPTER 2: THE ADJECTIVE 'MOVE' AND THE ADVERB 'MOVE'

"That's a what, Kristy? A bad question? All right, for Kristy's sake, let's rephrase that last question: what are the two verb functions? Okay? Satisfied?

*Linking verbs and Action verbs.*

3. What is the **adjective 'move'**?

*Tells more about words that have a noun function.*

4. What is the **first grammar piece** listed in **The Magical Wheel of Function** that does the **adjective 'move'**?

*Adjectives*

"And the answers please? Kristy, number 1?"

"The **noun** names something or someone."

"G-man, number 2?"

"The **linking verb** connects the subject and the predicate and the **action verb** shows the action in the sentence."

"Okay, and number 3, Felix? What's the adjective 'move'?"

"**Adjectives** tell more about words that have the **noun function**."

"What are you guys trying to do, put me out of a job? Very good! Okay, Giovanni, what do you have for number 4? What's the first grammar piece listed under the adjective 'move'?

"The adjective."

# LESSON 1: INTRODUCTION TO THE ADJECTIVE 'MOVE'

"Bingo-rama! That's where we're going today—**adjectives**, and they tell us more about nouns.

"Okay, let's go to work. In the next exercise we go on a fishing expedition for adjectives. You're what, Felix? Rusty on that—finding adjectives? Oh, boy! Well, did you forget about your adjective test? Try that out. It's on page 19."

**Exercise 1:** Underline all adjectives in the following sentences.

1. Kevin is the funniest student in the class.

2. Mr. Lund wears absurd ties.

3. I hate sarcastic people.

4. Yesterday I had a zillion problems.

5. That's what I call a boring movie.

6. I love huge cars.

7. He had two eggs in each pocket.

8. You look gorgeous.

9. Aren't you tired?

10. The coffee at the cafeteria is lousy.

## CHAPTER 2: THE ADJECTIVE 'MOVE' AND THE ADVERB 'MOVE'

"Did you have any trouble? The **Professional Clamdiggers** in the audience may have noticed that the 'adjective' test did not work too well on two of the adjectives in those sentences. Do you know which ones they are? Write them down. Don't try bluffing me. Of all people don't do that to me!"

"If you don't know what I'm talking about, don't worry about that yet. I'll tell you how to solve that problem in just a bit. First, let's talk about adjectives for a few minutes and then I'll let you worry a little more about those sentences. Kristy?"

"I think the problem is with #4 and #7."

"Okay, smarty pants. I knew you wanted to get that in there. And you're right.

"As you can see from the *Magical Wheel of Function* on page 14, an **adjective** does something to a word with the Noun function (a word that names **someone** or **something**). Well, what does it do, Giovanni?"

"I'm not sure, Mr. Lund."

"Well, hang on a minute and I'll tell you. What it does is change the picture of a noun. Now I'm going to prove to you how this works."

Quick, grab a pencil or pen! We're going to do an experiment. Look at this sentence. (Just look; don't ask me any questions yet, please. Thank you.)

I have a _____ car.

## LESSON 1: INTRODUCTION TO THE ADJECTIVE 'MOVE'

Okay, now here's the experiment. I'm going to fill in that blank and I want you to tell me what kind of car you see in your mind.

(You can write down the model and year or color of the car. Or, if you prefer, you can draw the car or attach a picture you've lifted from a magazine.)

A. I have a **junky** car.

This is what you imagine:

Okay now here's the second part of the exam—I mean experiment. (Heh, heh, just kidding!)

B. I have an **awesome** car.

Here's what you imagine:

Now are those two cars the same? Do you have the same picture for those two cars? No?

"What's the difference, Kristy?"

"The first one reminds me of my first boyfriend's car. It had duct tape on the front seat. The second one reminds me of my mother's new Prius."

## CHAPTER 2: THE ADJECTIVE 'MOVE' AND THE ADVERB 'MOVE'

"What? You're saying a Prius is an awesome car?"

"Okay, Giovanni. We're not arguing about cars. We're trying to figure out adjectives, and Kristy's right: the adjective changes the picture of the car. It changes the picture of the noun."

**Exercise 2**: Now go back up to the ten sentences in Exercise 1 and circle the noun (or picture) that is changed by the adjectives.

In fact, while you're at it, draw an arrow from the adjective to the noun that it is modifying.

| | Adjective | → | Noun |
|---|---|---|---|
| 1. | funniest | → | student |
| 2. | absurd | → | ties |
| 3. | sarcastic | → | people |
| 4. | zillion | → | problems |
| 5. | boring | → | move |
| 6. | huge | → | car |

LESSON 1: INTRODUCTION TO THE ADJECTIVE 'MOVE'

7. _____ two → eggs
   each → pocket

8. _____ gonpes → you

9. _____ tired → you

10. _____ lousy → coffee

---

So adjectives change the picture of nouns. Think of adjectives as a way to "Photoshop" nouns. Think of the cool things you can do with that: give your friend a cool new hair color, and, conversely, give premature baldness to the jerk who sits behind you in Health class.

---

HERE ARE THE FOUR
**ADJECTIVE QUESTIONS:**

1. **WHAT** kind of?

2. **WHICH** (one) or **WHOSE**?

3. **HOW MANY**\*?

4. **HOW** (if it comes after a Linking Verb)?

## CHAPTER 2: THE ADJECTIVE 'MOVE' AND THE ADVERB 'MOVE'

*This was the problem that Kristy said she had with sentences 4 and 7. Notice, the third type of information seems a little awkward when it is captured in our adjective test. For example in #4, "It is two" sounds kind of weird. You can resolve this by using "there" for your subject of the adjective test sentence.

For example:

There are two.            (#4 in exercise 1)
There are a zillion.      (#7 in exercise 1)

Or you can resolve it just by remembering that **how many** is an adjective question.

Please turn to the *Magical Wheel of Function* on page 14, and write these four questions neatly in the adjective piece of pie. Thank you.

Exercise 3: Now go back up to the ten sentences above. Over each adjective write **what kind of, which one** or **whose, how many, or how (after a Linking Verb)** so we know what information the adjective is giving us, how it is changing the picture of the adjective.

|    | Adjective | → | Question |
|----|-----------|---|----------|
| 1. | funniest  | → | which one |
| 2. | absurd    | → | what kind of |
| 3. | sarcastic | → | what kind of |

## LESSON 1: INTRODUCTION TO THE ADJECTIVE 'MOVE'

4. _____ zillion → how many

5. _____ boring → what kind of

6. _____ huge → what kind of

7. _____ two → how many
          each → which one

8. _____ gorgeous → how

9. _____ tired → how

10. _____ lousy → what kind of

**Check answers with your teacher please!**

---

Now, let's have a little fun. Do you like to draw? Good. (Whether you do or don't doesn't matter.)

**Exercise 4**: Draw two pictures of girls and two pictures of guys. (Please make your drawings kind of primitive and funny because I'm not very artistic and I don't want to look bad.) Then write a sentence next to each picture. Use adjectives that fit your picture, or better yet draw pictures that fit your adjectives. Ex: My girlfriend Denise is very athletic. (Put some good triceps

## CHAPTER 2: THE ADJECTIVE 'MOVE' AND THE ADVERB 'MOVE'

and biceps on that one.) Get it? Go for it!

Write four sentences and draw four pictures. Remember, please make them primitive and funny- or stupid-looking.

1. My crazy friend loves to eat big rocks.

2. Her big feet were extremely gross and deskusting.

3. He is thinking very deeply.

LESSON 1: INTRODUCTION TO THE ADJECTIVE 'MOVE'

4. She is so old, she's pratically aching.

**Bring your artwork to class tomorrow. That's all folks!**

CHAPTER 2: THE ADJECTIVE 'MOVE' AND THE ADVERB 'MOVE'

# Lesson 2: Why the Heck Do We Need Adjectives and Where Do They Go?

"Now before we go any further, let me show you a trick or two about finding ....What did you say, Giovanni? What kind of question is that? Why do we need adjectives? You want me to answer that? Really? Have I told you, G-man, that you can be a little difficult at times?

"Let's see ... if I can show you why ... ah ... we use adjectives. Yes, of course, I'm stalling. Okay. I got it."

**Exercise 5**: Think of your favorite vacation place, okay? Got it? Okay, now tell me all about it, say in about **fifty words**. Wait a minute—one more thing. **No adjectives**! That's right. You heard me right: **you cannot use any adjectives**. Quit stalling and do it!

*The beach has sand, water and sun. The beach also has shrimp, lobsters and crab to eat. It also has fishing, skeying, and bouts. There is also dolfins, fish and sharks. There are hoetells with pools and casinos. The beach also has jellyfish, jetskeys, and subs. My vacation is at the beach.*

# LESSON 2: WHY THE HECK DO WE NEED ADJECTIVES?

Okay, now I have a feeling you want to tell me something, and so the complaint department is now officially open.

> Write out five complaints you have about this exercise. Try to start your complaint with the words **I feel**. For example: When I write without adjectives, I feel . . .

1. When I write without adjectives, I feel challenged.

2. When I write without adjectives, I feel like it always is just naming things.

3. When I write without adjectives, I feel like it doesn't make much sense.

4. When I write without adjectives, I feel dum.

5. When I write without adjectives, I feel like some things missing.

Ouf-da! That's Norwegian for ay yai yai, which is Italian for Heavens to Betsy. You are an unhappy camper, aren't you? Would you like to leave this alone for awhile and come back to it next year when you feel a bit stronger? No? That's good.

# CHAPTER 2: THE ADJECTIVE 'MOVE' AND THE ADVERB 'MOVE'

**Exercise 5B:** All right, now rewrite that paragraph about your favorite vacation place, and you now have my permission to use any adjectives you want. Remember, fifty words or so.

> The beach is the best place to go on vacation. There is so much to do like swiming, skeying, or even building a sand castle. There is also lots of great food like shrimp, lobster, and crab. The sunset is always great, and you can't miss out on berekfist it is Just the best.

Now how did it feel to be able to use adjectives again? What was the difference? Okay, Giovanni, I think you just answered your own question. Get the picture?

"All right, now back to the tips for finding . . . what, Felix? You now know why we have adjectives, but why do we have to study them? You're full of questions today, aren't you, Mr. Felix? Have you noticed that Kristy never asks me questions like that? So what? That's your response to a reasonable question? All right, let me try to solve that by giving you eine kleine qvizz (that means a little quiz). Circle the letter of the correct answer.

1. (a.) I don't feel well today.
   (b.) I don't feel good today.

2. How are you?
   a. I'm pretty well.
   (b.) I'm pretty good.

## LESSON 2: WHY THE HECK DO WE NEED ADJECTIVES?

Yes, I know. You're stuck, aren't you? Heh, heh. Not feeling too good (slash) well yourself, eh Giovanni? Well, my friend—that's precisely **why you need to study adjectives and adverbs.** When you master this chapter (as, of course, you will), you will know the answer to those and other problems that have kept you from being the self-confident Professional Clamdigger you've always dreamed of being. Okay, now can I show you some tricks for finding adjectives? Thank you very much.

Adjectives are found in two places in sentences:

1. **Adjective** Noun
(before the noun)

2. Linking Verb **Adjective**
(after a linking verb)

"That's it?"

"That's it, Giovanni!"

"Nowhere else?"

"Nowhere else. You don't believe me? All right, let's try it out."

Wait a minute. Wait a minute. I just thought of something. You DO remember the linking verbs, don't you? You need to know that to do this exercise. Oh yeah? Write 'em out right below before you do the exercise.

# CHAPTER 2: THE ADJECTIVE 'MOVE' AND THE ADVERB 'MOVE'

**Write out the 13 linking verbs below:**

1. Be
2. Appears
3. Seems
4. Looks
5. Smells
6. Sounds
7. Taste
8. Feels
9. Stay
10. Remain
11. Grow
12. Become
13. Get

## LESSON 2: WHY THE HECK DO WE NEED ADJECTIVES?

**Exercise 6**: Look at the following sentences. Circle the adjectives in the sentences, then tell me where you found the adjective by putting **before noun** or **after linking verb** over the adjective.

1. Our (soccer) team has (blue) uniforms.   before noun / before noun
2. Everybody seems (tired) today.   after linking verb
3. That (sounded) (strange).   before noun ? / after linking verb
4. This chair is not (comfortable).   after linking verb
5. My cat has (gray) fur.   before noun
6. The (first) person to arrive in class was Paul.   before noun
7. This is (irritating).   after linking verb
8. That cologne smells (awful).   after linking verb
9. Take the (second) towel, please.   before noun
10. We're visiting a (gorgeous) lake in East Texas.   before noun
11. You can load (three) CDs at a time.   before noun
12. That's (my) car in the garage.   before noun

# CHAPTER 2: THE ADJECTIVE 'MOVE' AND THE ADVERB 'MOVE'

**Exercise 7:** Any trouble? Now write in the type of information that the adjective is adding to the sentences above. Remember the four question types? (If not, see page 79)

1. what kind of
2. how
3. how
4. what kind of / How
5. whose / what kind of
6. whose / which one
7. how
8. how
9. how many / which one
10. whose / what kind of

Check your answers with your teacher, amigos. Adios.

# Lesson 3: The Adverb 'move'

"The last grammar 'move' I have to teach you is…."

"Wait, wait, wait…just one minute. Did you say the last grammar 'move'? We're only in chapter two and we're already learning the last grammar 'move,' Mr. Lund?"

"That's right, the LAST grammar 'move'!!!! In fact you have already seen it; it's on your *Magical Wheel of Function* on page 14. Go and check to see what it is. And while you're at it, how many major grammar 'moves' are there in the English language? Got it, Kristy? What are they?"

"There are four 'moves': the noun 'move," the verb 'move,' the adjective 'move,' and the adverb 'move.'"

"Okay, another piece of watermelon for the modest Ms. Kristy. And today we are going to study the LAST grammar 'move' in English—**the adverb 'move.'**"

Now I imagine that you think you know what an adverb looks like, right? Right. Okay, let's take eine kleine qvizz (translation: a little quiz) on this.

---

### POP QUIZ!

Directions: Circle the correct answer(s):

    **A.** Adverbs end in -ly.
    **B.** Adverbs do not end in -ly.

---

## CHAPTER 2: THE ADJECTIVE 'MOVE' AND THE ADVERB 'MOVE'

"Did you answer A? You're wrong. Did you answer B? You're wrong! The answer is actually **A AND B**. I know, I know. You learned in 5th grade that **all adverbs end in -ly** and you studied that statement until you had it committed to memory. Nice job! CLAP, CLAP, CLAP, CLAP (Or if you prefer a golf clap: clap, clap, clap, clap, clap.) And now you can't believe that that's not right. Well, let's say it's almost right. (Don't forget. Are you paying me to make you a professional clamdigger or bush-league clamdigger?) Yes, true. Most adverbs do end in -ly.

**Example:** The beauty and the beast lived happily ever after.

"'**Happily**' is an adverb, yes, yes, true, but so is '**ever after.**' (Easy, easy, DON'T, I repeat, DO NOT close this book. This is just a warm-up, a tease, if you want to call it that. I haven't TAUGHT you anything about adverbs yet. Remember this IS the last move you have to learn.)

"Furthermore—to have just a bit more fun with you—**there are some -ly words that are not adverbs.** Example: find the adverb in the following sentence:

    **Drive friendly.**

"Do you see one, Mr. Felix Navidad?"

    "Yeah, it's 'friendly.'"

"I wish it were, my friend. **Friendly** is not an adverb (and that sentence, by the way, is not a grammatical sentence even though it is plastered all over Texas highways). **Friendly is an adjective**."

Here are a few other **-ly** adjectives: **daily** bath, **early** morning, **kindly** grandmother, **homely** dog (homely means **ugly**, oops there's another one), **lovely** tea (the British use tea and lovely more than Americans do). By the way, if you don't believe me, put the adjective test on any of those adjectives.

# LESSON 3: THE ADVERB 'MOVE'

**What are the adjective questions?**

1. *what kind of*
2. *whose or which*
3. *How many*
4. *How*

Oh, well. The point of all this is to show you that our 5th grade lessons will not get us through the fourth and last move—the adverb move. Okay? Get the picture? Now, are you ready to study it?

The adverb changes the picture on what other words? See your *Magical Wheel of Function* on page 14 for help.

That's right. The **adverb** changes the picture (or modifies) verbs, adjectives and other adverbs. Busy little beaver, isn't it? Okay, you can learn it that way, or if you're like me and like to learn the least information necessary to do the job, you can think of it this way: What does an adjective modify?

_____

"Did you say **nouns or pronouns**, Giovanni? I may have to adopt you one of these days. Wonderful! Okay, then **adverbs modify everything else**: verbs, adjectives, and adverbs. That's it, right? All the moves? If you find any more moves on the function wheel, I'll buy you sixteen dozen orders of fries at Quickie Burger. No, not cheese fries. That would be too much cholesterol for your delicate system. Make yourself a big note in the right-hand margin. **Adjectives** modify nouns and **Adverbs** modify all the other pieces. You do know all the other pieces right? Right? RIGHT? Okay, what are they?"

## CHAPTER 2: THE ADJECTIVE 'MOVE' AND THE ADVERB 'MOVE'

*All right, roll up your sleeves now. Let's look at some examples of adverbs and let's go to work. (Please everyone—not just Kristy—notice that the adverbs are in CAPS.)*

1. Mr. Lund speaks German SLOWLY.

2. Mr. Lund speaks German EVERYWHERE in his house.

3. Mr. Lund can't speak German EARLY in the morning.

4. Mr. Lund can ALMOST speak German.

*Exercise 8*: Now see if you can come up with the questions that adverbs answer. Notice there is a prepositional phrase in two of the sentences. **Cross them out** as usual (until next chapter) so they don't confuse you.

1. How
2. Where
3. When
4. To what extent

LESSON 3: THE ADVERB 'MOVE'

# Professional Clamdigging™ Mastery Rule:

## Adverb Question Mastery Rule

**Here are the QUESTIONS FOR ADVERBS:**

**1. HOW**
(after an action verb or before an adjective or adverb) does he speak German? How well does he speak? How hard is German?

**2. WHERE**
does he speak German?

**3. WHEN**
does he speak German?

**4. TO WHAT EXTENT**
does he speak German?

**Exercise 9**: Okay, I think we're ready for an adverb hunting expedition. Find the adverbs in each sentence and underline them. Then above the adverb write the question that it answers.

1. My friend can <u>really</u> *(How)* cook Italian food.

2. <u>Today</u> *(When)* I'm teaching you about the adverb move.

3. I <u>never</u> *(When)* eat internal organs.

# CHAPTER 2: THE ADJECTIVE 'MOVE' AND THE ADVERB 'MOVE'

4. I looked everywhere for my glasses. [where]

5. We are expecting company Monday. [when]

6. The accident unexpectedly changed my plans. [To what extent]

7. The president spoke passionately about the Peace Corps. [How]

---

**Exercise 10:** The **adverbs** in Exercise 9 all modified verbs. Now we are going to mix in the other words that adverbs modify. Find the adverbs in the following sentences and draw an arrow to the word that it modifies. Then put in the question word.

1. Professional Clamdiggers can learn almost anything.

2. She is a really good dancer.

3. She is indeed a semi-professional Clamdigger.

4. I certainly am happy to see you again.

5. My car is terribly dirty.

6. The two teams were exactly equal in terms of penalties.

7. Christopher improvises amazingly well on the keyboard.

# LESSON 3: THE ADVERB 'MOVE'

"What did you say, Felix? This is harder than the adjective move, isn't it? I know, I know. Do you want to lie down for a few minutes? Aspirin? No? Hard on your tummy? Oh, that's too bad. Do you want me to remind you why we're doing this?"

**Which of the two sentences is correct?**

I feel good.
I feel well.

**Or how about these?** (heh, heh)

I feel bad.
I feel badly.

**The answer is coming up in the next lesson. Later 'gator.**

Seriously, are you feeling okay? You look a little white around the gills, my fellow fish mates. I think you need to take a stroll around the block. That means walk, not drive.

CHAPTER 2: THE ADJECTIVE 'MOVE' AND THE ADVERB 'MOVE'

# Lesson 4: Which is Which? Adjective/Adverb Forms

Good morning, Clamdiggers. Do you know your **adjective move**? Tell me about it. What is the adjective move? Need some help to get started?

**Where do we find adjectives?**
Before the noun or after a linking verb

**What pictures do they change or, if you prefer, what words do they modify?**
_____

**What questions do they answer?**
What, which one, or whose, how many, How

Okay, now how about the **adverb move**?

**What pictures do they change (which words do they modify)?**
_____

**What questions do they answer?**
How, Where, When, To what extent

"Okay, now we're ready to do something with all of this wonderful info .... NOW what is it, Giovanni? Go ahead. You'll feel better when you get it off your chest."

"Look, Mr. Lund. I'm sorry and all that, but I can't help it. It's great and wonderful to fill out all these answers, but I still keep wanting to know—

## LESSON 4: WHICH IS WHICH? ADJECTIVE/ADVERB FORMS

what's the point of all this—adjective moves, adjective questions, adverb moves, adverb questions?"

"Tell me the truth, G-force. You had a rough night last night, didn't you? You didn't get enough sleep; I can tell. You know what happens when you don't get enough sleep? Things just do not click! And now you're trying to take it out on me, aren't you? No, wait a minute. Maybe I didn't get enough sleep. All right, all right, I'll try to answer your question."

But first I want to ask you to do one simple thing. Read the following sentence and circle the correct answers. (You noticed, eh? I always give eine kleine qvizz when I'm under stress. So, what do you do—brush your teeth? Pet your pet turtle? Sing raps to your dog?)

**Exercise 11**: Circle the correct words in the following sentence:

John looked (cold, *coldly*) at the waiter and then said,

"My broccoli looks (*cold*, coldly)."

"Now, speaking of baseball.... you all know how to play baseball, right? Let's say you and I are in an argument because your favorite batter has just been called out on strikes. You say the last pitch was a ball, and I, a fan for the opposing team, say no way, Jose; that was a strike. He's outta there.

"Now we're having a heavy duty argument about this pitch, and, let's say, someone comes along and says well, what is the difference between a ball and a strike?"

What would you say? Go ahead and write it down. Don't ask me; you're the baseball expert."

*A ball is when the ball is outside the box and they don't swing anything else is a strike.*

# CHAPTER 2: THE ADJECTIVE 'MOVE' AND THE ADVERB 'MOVE'

It is pretty complicated when you get right down to it, isn't it? A strike is a ball thrown which touches an area as wide as the plate and which is no higher than the letters of the batter (whatever that means) and no lower than his knees (and of course the ball is only traveling 110 miles an hour so that shouldn't hurt our ability to make the right call). You see what I mean?

Even in something as simple as a ball or strike call there are very complex and complicated rules governing our judgment. Now back to poor John and the poor waiter. Did you put **John looked (cold or coldly) at the waiter** and why? Now most amateur Clamdiggers would look at that sentence and a nebulous cloud would begin to form in their minds and they might say, hey I have an idea. "Let's see, I bet cold is an adjective and coldly is an adverb and that's wonderful and brilliant thinking (5th grade thinking), but the teacher is still waiting for the answer. The problem here is this:

Is **look** in this sentence a *linking verb* (I told you you'd hear that word again) or an *action verb*?"
*action verb*

If it is a **linking verb**, what word will follow?
*cold*

If it is an **action verb** what word will follow?
*coldly*

## LESSON 4: WHICH IS WHICH? ADJECTIVE/ADVERB FORMS

**If it were winter in Minnesota and John had just left the minus 20 degree weather outside and entered the restaurant, we could say that John looked cold.** Why?

*Because he looked* _____

Yes, because **look** in this case is a **linking verb** and the linking verb would be completed by an **ADJECTIVE** and not an ADVERB. But in this case John is looking at the waiter (a person, hopefully, and not a vegetable) and so we say,

"How is he looking at the waiter?"

"Coldly."

"Yes, thank you, Felix. You know, you're getting quite good at this. Now how did you know that? Because you know that **how** is an adverb question (after an action verb) and not an adjective question, and you know that it is modifying an action verb which adverbs and not adjectives modify, and therefore you need to choose the adverb form **coldly** which you have known since 5th grade and probably since you were born and so that's the answer.

"But imagine if you didn't know all that seemingly useless information about **adverb moves, adverb questions, adjective moves and adjective questions**? You'd be like a Pakistani who sat down next to you and me at the ball game (he got off at the wrong bus stop) and overheard our argument about the last pitch and wondered how does one even know if a pitch is a strike or a ball? Okay? Any other questions? I didn't think so."

"Now, you analyze the second part of the **John** sentence—Kristy?"

"My broccoli looks cold."

That's right, it should be **cold** because broccoli is incapable of action (as far as I know) and so the verb is a linking verb and requires an adjective. Got it?

## CHAPTER 2: THE ADJECTIVE 'MOVE' AND THE ADVERB 'MOVE'

So here we go:

John looked coldly at the waiter and then said, "My broccoli looks cold."

"Now do you understand why you have felt like you were moving into a cloud when you walked into an English grammar class discussion? Like they were speaking a foreign language? It's the rules, man. Learn the rules. **Don't let the Professional Clamdiggers have all the fun!**

# Professional Clamdigging™ Mastery Rule:

### Mastery Rule for Choosing Adjectives and Adverbs

**Linking Verbs** go with **Adjectives**.
**Action Verbs** go with **Adverbs**.

**Exercise 12**: Do the following sentences in two steps:

A. Circle the verb. Decide if it is a LV or an AcV and write one of those abbreviations above the verb.

# LESSON 4: WHICH IS WHICH? ADJECTIVE/ADVERB FORMS

B. **Remember**: *adjectives* go with LVs and *adverbs* go with AcVs. Choose the **CORRECT** word in parentheses. Write that at the top of the next page to help you on the exercise.

**WARNING: one of the problems cannot be solved using the directions above. More on that later.**

1. The orange juice tasted [LV] (**bitter**/bitterly).

2. I was feeling [LV] (bad/**badly**) about the rejection letter.

3. Alex never does [AcV] his homework on a (**regular**/regularly) [AcV] basis.

4. Chris does [AcV] his homework (regular/**regularly**).

5. The tissue smelled [LV] (fragrant/**fragrantly**).

6. The dog jumped [AcV] (wild/**wildly**) when I let him go.

7. Sir, please speak [AcV] more (slow/**slowly**).

8. Why are you feeling [LV] so (**sad**/sadly)?

9. Hold the steering [AcV] wheel (firm/**firmly**).

10. I'm really feeling [LV] (**bad**/badly) today.

11. Your stereo sounded [LV] (**wonderful**/wonderfully) last night.

12. Courtney is [LV] (**fabulous**/fabulously).

## CHAPTER 2: THE ADJECTIVE 'MOVE' AND THE ADVERB 'MOVE'

Did you find the problem that cannot be solved using my directions? Which is it? Did you say #3? The problem here is this. Do you remember I told you that an adjective can appear in **two** places?

> Two adjective positions in a sentence:
>
> 1. Mr. Couser is <u>smart</u>. (After a LV)
> 2. That is a <u>terrific</u> hamburger. (Before a Noun)

"Now look at the parenthesis in #3. Is it in position 1 or 2, Giovanni?"

"It's like sentence #2."

"That's right. And what word is it modifying, G-Man?"

"Basis."

"So which word do we choose?"

"Regular."

"Very good, Jove. It is modifying the noun **basis**. Therefore, we need to choose the adjective **regular**, not the adverb **regularly**.

"Now look at #6. Try that one, Kristy."

"That is a case where the word is modifying the Action Verb and requires the adverb **regularly**."

"Correct!"

"I have a question for you, Mr. Lund."

## LESSON 4: WHICH IS WHICH? ADJECTIVE/ADVERB FORMS

"Okay, Kristy; fire away."

**Which is correct:** I am (real/(really)) tired.

"I was afraid you were going to ask that one, Kristy. Here is where I have to put my *Standard written English "Cap"* on and say that 'real' is very common in our everyday speech, but it is considered an informal use. **The best answer is "really." That is the adverb form.**

And, by the way, this is only the second or third time in this book, I believe, that I have made the distinction between what is commonly said in conversation (colloquial or informal or conversational English) and Standard written English. That is where you need to start to develop your own instincts about what is the best thing to say.

And, in case you didn't know it, we all have different levels of English that we will bring to different tasks and audiences. You will probably choose words and grammar more carefully when you are applying for a job with a stranger than when you are hanging out with friends in the lunch room. Actually, the dirty secret is that we often choose informal language when we are with friends and more formal language in more formal situations to "fit in" with the people we are talking to.

---

But **do not hear me say**
that "It doesn't matter in grammar: anything goes, anything is okay."
No! That is not true!

My main argument in this book is that **Standard English**
is the **default style** for your writing.

---

## CHAPTER 2: THE ADJECTIVE 'MOVE' AND THE ADVERB 'MOVE'

"Felix, did you have anything to eat for breakfast? Could you try to control those noises coming from your stomach? Thank you, my friend."

I can take a hint. Go to lunch, you guys. And by the way, we are having a very important guest tomorrow. Dress your best, and in fact, bring your dancing shoes. It is going to be party central around here tomorrow. I've worked you guys hard enough; it's time to have a little fun—enjoy grammar—I mean life!—a little.

# Lesson 5: James Brown Has Arrived with that Answer!

Okay, my friends, I think we're ready for the $64,000 question. Remember what it is?

Which is correct?

A. I feel well.
B. I feel good.

There's only one piece of information you need to know in order to settle this kind of problem for the rest of your life. Do you know what that is?

Here it is. Are you ready? Are you sure? There's no going back now once I give you the information; you realize that, don't you? You can't just shrug your shoulders and go uh-uh anymore when this problem comes up. You will have a moral obligation to give the correct information to anyone who is interested. That is the solemn oath of the Professional Clamdigger. All right? You agreed?

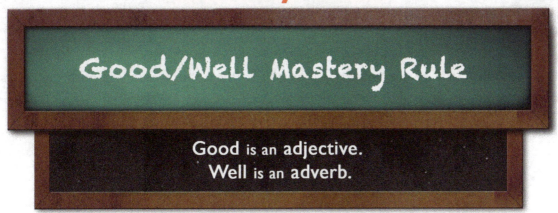

## CHAPTER 2: THE ADJECTIVE 'MOVE' AND THE ADVERB 'MOVE'

Ahhhhhhh! Now don't you feel better already? That's it. Okay, now go back up to the problem before and decide on the best answer—write down an airtight and watertight argument about why the one you chose is correct. Write out your argument here:

"Okay, who wants to do this? Giovanni, come on down! What's the story here please for goodness' sakes? Finally, let's get it solved!"

> "Well, you said that 'good' is an adjective and that 'well' is an adverb, and we know that the verb 'feel' is a linking verb, and we know that the linking verb is modified by an adjective, so…"

"Yes, yes? You're doing great, Mr. Giovanni. Keep going. Don't fall asleep at the wheel. Don't text and drive either."

> "So that means that the correct sentence is: **I feel good.**"

"So do I, Giovanni; I feel good too, now that I've heard your answer. You are one smart dude. And you know what, everybody? It is time to break it out and celebrate this **milestone in our grammar education**. And to do that I have invited a guest lecturer who is going to get the party started.

[CUE THE YOUTUBE RECORDING OF JAMES BROWN, "I feel good." And please play the recorded—not the live version. Just look for an album cover on YouTube. AND PLEASE **CRANK IT LOUD!**]

I tell you what: let's let our "visiting professor" do the honors. First let's push the chairs out of the way so we have some room to dance.

LESSON 5: JAMES BROWN HAS ARRIVED WITH THAT ANSWER!

# MISTER JAMES BROWN!

**[KEEP THE MUSIC GOING FOR THE REST OF THE LESSON PLEASE!]**

(Photograph courtesy of David King)

By the way, if you were not lucky enough to live in the 60s like I did, you may not be lucky enough to know about James Brown, master of R&B and soul music and funky stuff too. Here we go, and feel free to get up and move around. Here's a few dance steps that we used to do back in the day: The Twist, **The Mash Potatoes**, *The Monkey*, The Monster Mash, **The Bugaloo**, *The Watusi*, The Pony, **The Hitch Hike**, **The Swim**, *The Skate*, and the **The Freddie**. And did I mention *the Jerk*, **the Pony**, and **Locomotion**? (I'm sure there were more but that's all we heard about in my hometown Chicago.)

## CHAPTER 2: THE ADJECTIVE 'MOVE' AND THE ADVERB 'MOVE'

If you don't know any of those dances, then just go ahead and do whatever makes you feel (What?—good or well?) Everybody!

"Can't hear you!"

# "OH SORRY! IS IT, 'I FEEL GOOD OR WELL'?"

"I feel **good**!"

[Finish the tune.]

(Photograph courtesy of Michael Strong)

## LESSON 5: JAMES BROWN HAS ARRIVED WITH THAT ANSWER!

Okay, whew! I don't know about you guys, but at my age that's about all the fun that my heart can handle. For tonight your homework is to find a video rendition of one of those dances—and bonus if you learn to do it to the James Brown tune. But most of all, your homework is to **celebrate the fact that you can answer the question that an overwhelming majority of Americans cannot!**

**CHAPTER 2: THE ADJECTIVE 'MOVE' AND THE ADVERB 'MOVE'**

# Lesson 6: "Good" and "Well"— One Parting Shot

"Okay, Kristy—did you do any dance research?"

"Yeah, actually, I found a video on 60s dancing and my favorite was the Temptation Walk."

"Are you going to show us?"

"No thanks, Mr. Lund! I don't think anyone of us wants to compete with that picture of you in the last chapter."

"All right, I'll let you off the hook on that one, Kristy. By the way, I like the looks of that Party Rock dance and can't figure that one out. Anyone want some major extra credit—Giovanni? You give me some lessons on Party Rock and I give you. . . no? Don't know it? Okay, we'll let's get back to business.

Coming up is a Professional Clamdigging™ tip. Jump to * if you want to skip it, but, on the other hand, if you want to dazzle your friends and teachers with your grammatical acumen for the rest of your life, here it is (and I want you all to join me there—Felix, Giovanni, AND Kristy):

Oh hi, Felix, hi Giovanni, hi Kristy. Glad you hung around this time. Ahem. I don't exactly know how to tell you this ... but ... ah ... well ... yes, it is possible to say "I feel well" but only in this one limited context. (waitaminutedon'tinterruptmelistenandI'llexplain)

## LESSON 6: "GOOD" AND "WELL" — ONE PARTING SHOT

Hey, Mr. Lund. How are you feeling today? You didn't look too **good** yesterday.

Thank you, Kristy. Yeah, I was pretty sick yesterday, but I feel quite **well** today, thanks.

Do you have any idea why we can do this? Write your answer here:
_____

Do you want me to tell you the answer and spoil all your fun? Of course? What kind of answer is that, Giovanni? Okay, I'll write out the answer **under the money signs below.** If you want to show me your answer tomorrow without looking at mine, skip down to the *.

"Here's a hint: what kind of word is **sick**, Kristy?"

"**Sick** is an **adjective**."

"Okay, then, my **Clamdigger** fiends—I mean—friends. Here is the moment of truth. There is another adjective meaning the opposite of **sick**.

### FOR 899 THOUSAND, FOUR HUNDRED AND THIRTEEN DOLLARS, WHAT IS IT?

$$$$$$$$$$$$$$$$$$$$$$$$$$$$$$$$$$$$$$$$$$$$$$$$$$$

It's ... ah ... well, ... that's right—**well**.

Confused? That's not surprising. You should be. Look!

**Well** is an *adverb* in the following sentence. (Notice it is used in contrast with **good** which is the *adjective* form.) Look at sentences A and B below.

# CHAPTER 2: THE ADJECTIVE 'MOVE' AND THE ADVERB 'MOVE'

A. This bat is really **good**.

B. You bat very **well** (for an old man, Mr. Lund).

---- **BUT** ----

**Well** is an adjective in the following sentence where it means healthy or not sick.

Dr. Kildare, how is your patient today? She's perfectly **well**, thank you.

Get it?

---- <u>well</u> ≠ <u>well</u> ----

(Of course this is true with many words in English. **Do** is not the same as **do** in the following: **Do** you **do** your homework every night? The first **do** is a helping verb, the second **do** is an action verb.)

How many times do I have to tell you—don't look at *me*. I didn't invent this language. I'm trying to figure it out, just like you are.

Okay, that's enough amusement. Now let's get to work. Here's an exercise to let you know if you are on the way to becoming a master. (Your mastery exam is coming up in two or three days, by the way.)

## LESSON 6: "GOOD" AND "WELL" — ONE PARTING SHOT

**Exercise 13**: Directions: complete the following sentences in two steps.

A. Circle the verb and decide if it is a LV or an AcV and write the correct abbreviation above the verb.

B. Use your knowledge about "pieces" (adjectives go with LVs and adverbs go with AcVs) to choose the CORRECT word in parentheses

1. The soccer team *AcV* played (good/**well**) today.

2. Jill and I *AcV* worked very (good/**well**) together.

3. Renee *LV* is a (well/**good**) bowler.

4. She *AcV* knows me too (good/**well**).

5. My shirts never *AcV* fit me too (good/**well**).

6. My brother really *LV* looks (**good**/well) in a tuxedo.

7. Unfortunately, Chicago *AcV* did very (bad/**badly**) at the regional tournament.

8. My friend Jimmy *AcV* thinks that mustard goes (good/**well**) with french fries.

9. Hey, Pete. Did you *LV* do (good/**well**) on that Clamdigging quiz today?

10. I can't go to the football game because I'm *LV* not (good/**well**) at the moment.

11. If the food *LV* smells (**bad**/badly), throw it away.

12. Your grades didn't *LV* sound too (**good**/well) to me.

## CHAPTER 2: THE ADJECTIVE 'MOVE' AND THE ADVERB 'MOVE'

13. That dessert tasted so (good)/well) that I can't resist fourths.

14. You sure don't treat your friends very (good/(well)).

15. I understand Spanish pretty (good/(well)).

# Lesson 7: Using Commas with Multiple Adjectives

The last section before the mastery test on Adjective and Adverb moves gives me great pleasure: an introduction to your *first mastery comma rule*. Put your thinking caps on. This one is a thinker. Here it is:

## Professional Clamdigging™ Mastery Rule:

### Coordinate Adjective Mastery Comma Rule

Use commas between two or more (coordinate) adjectives in a sentence.

### Professional Clamdigging™ Memory Sentence
Coordinate Adjective Sentence

She is my warm, witty wife.

## CHAPTER 2: THE ADJECTIVE 'MOVE' AND THE ADVERB 'MOVE'

Example 1: Equal/Coordinate adjectives (COMMA)

**She is my <u>warm, witty</u> wife.**

**warm = witty**

Example 2: Unequal/Non-coordinate adjectives (NO COMMA)

**The room was full of <u>loud freshmen</u> students.**

**loud ≠ freshmen**

You see in Example 1, the two adjectives **warm** and **witty** are roughly equal in importance. Therefore, we say they are **coordinate adjectives** and require a comma between them.

In Example 2, however, **loud** and **freshmen** are really not equal. **Freshmen** gives the truer picture of the students. **Loud** is more of their condition at the moment. Therefore, the adjectives are **non-coordinate** and there are no commas between them.

(If you are confused, please don't despair. I have some tips below that will make this much easier. This explanation was designed to give you the basics as a starting point.)

### Professional Clamdigging Tip

One way to see if the adjectives are coordinate (equal) is to change their positions. If you can do this without changing the meaning and there is no 'strangeness' in either version, then they are equal or coordinate adjectives and **require a comma between them.**

### LESSON 7: USING COMMAS WITH MULTIPLE ADJECTIVES

1. She is my wonderful, delightful wife. (needs a comma!)

2. She is my delightful, wonderful wife. (needs a comma!)

**Professional Clamdigging Tip**

Another way to check for coordinate adjectives is to see if they still make sense if you join them with the word 'and.'

1. She is my wonderful and delightful wife.
2. She is my delightful and wonderful wife.

"Do they sound okay to you, Kristy?

"Yeah, and I notice that now we don't need a comma when we insert the word 'and' in either sentence."

"Correctomania. Let's try this together with a new sentence. How about you Felix? Are you getting this?"

"I think so, although nobody ever told me that you had to use commas with adjectives."

"Okay, Felix Navidad, come on down and get ready to play for the big bucks. Are you ready? Here's your sentence, buddy."

I have a brown wool suit.

## CHAPTER 2: THE ADJECTIVE 'MOVE' AND THE ADVERB 'MOVE'

"What do you say. Felix baby—commas or no commas? The whole world is watching. Don't be nervous or you'll be executed on the spot!*

(*That's a line from <u>Alice in Wonderland</u>, by the way.)

> "Uh, well. . . first of all, I think the adjectives are not equal or coordinate because you cannot reverse them."

"Try it! Let's hear it!

> *I have a **wool brown** suit.

"What do you think, Giovanni?"

> "Ngngxxxxxuhhhhhhh!"

"Okay, so do we use a comma or not? We're about to run out of air-time, man!"

> "No comma, Mr. Lund."

"Give that man a fajita salad. You've got ice water running in your veins, Felix. I'm proud of you."

(*the asterisk, by the way, indicates that the red sentence above is not correct, so that no one thinks that the publisher made a mistake.)

"Let's do one more and this one goes to Krisssssssssssty! Are you ready? I'll take that head nod for a yes! Here's your sentence."

> I like your baby blue eyes.

> "That's easy—no commas, Mr. Lund!"

LESSON 7: USING COMMAS WITH MULTIPLE ADJECTIVES

"Explain yourself please!"

"Well, for one thing, you can't say 'blue baby eyes.' Also, you can't say 'baby and blue eyes,' and 'baby' modifies the adjective 'blue' rather than the noun 'eyes.'"

Very interesting, Kristy just stumbled on . . . .

If you have coordinate adjectives, they must both (or all) modify or change the picture of the noun.
See the following examples A and B.

**Example A:** coordinate (equal) adjectives
She is my **wonderful** wife. (both adjectives modify the noun 'wife')
      **delightful**

**Example B:** non-coordinate (unequal)
I like her **baby** **blue** eyes ('baby' modifies 'blue' and 'blue' modifies 'eyes')

"What word does 'baby' modify in that last sentence, Giovanni?"

    "It modifies 'blue'?"

"And what kind of word is 'blue,' pray tell?"

    "It is an adjective."

# CHAPTER 2: THE ADJECTIVE 'MOVE' AND THE ADVERB 'MOVE'

"And what kind of word modifies an adjective, Kristy?"

"An adverb."

"So 'baby' is an adverb in this sentence?"

"Yes, it is, Mr. Lund."

"Comma or no comma?"

"No comma! We don't even have two adjectives together, let alone coordinate adjectives that need a comma."

"Wow! That's right! Any questions? My friends, we are a long way from where we were the day that we started this journey to Damascus. You guys are on your way to becoming **Professional Clamdiggers."**

> **Exercise 14**: Punctuate the following sentences using the Coordinate Adjective rule. Be sure you underline the adjectives and then put the word Coordinate in front of the sentence if the adjectives are coordinate and Non-Coordinate if they are not coordinate. Then put in commas as necessary.

1. We came home on a <u>rough</u> <u>muddy</u> road.
   _Coordinate_
2. The school just built a <u>new</u> <u>indoor</u> pool.
   _Coordinate_
3. The <u>noisy</u> senior class has off-campus lunch today.
   _non-coordinate_
4. My grandmother lives in a <u>dark</u> <u>brown</u> house.
   _coordinate_

## LESSON 7: USING COMMAS WITH MULTIPLE ADJECTIVES

5. Alex is the most <u>congenial, popular</u> person in the school.
   _coordinate_
6. The <u>greedy, brutal</u> gang members grew up to be malevolent members of the drug cartel.
   _coordinate_
7. My late mother was a very <u>caring, loving</u> person.
   _coordinate_
8. Joe is an <u>insidious</u> <u>unkempt</u> <u>dour</u> fellow.
   _coordinate_

**Check your answers and then move on to the next exercise.**

> **Exercise 15:** Now you write **four** sentences: **two** of which have multiple, coordinate adjectives (like the ones I just put in that sentence –#8–and be sure you put in commas!) and two of which have multiple, noncoordinating adjectives.

1. _Steve is my best, funniest friend._

2. _They have a dark, green apartment_

3. _The smelly eight year olds went on a field trip._

4. _The cool Jr's class got tacos for lunch._

**My friends, get ready for a mastery test tomorrow
on punctuating coordinate adjectives.**

# CHAPTER 2: THE ADJECTIVE 'MOVE' AND THE ADVERB 'MOVE'

**Exercise 16**: Chapter 2 Review—Are You Still With Me?

1. What is the noun function?
   _____
   _____

2. What is the adjective function?
   _____
   _____

3. What is the purpose of adjectives?
   _____
   _____

4. What are the four questions adjectives can answer?
   Write out original sentences to illustrate each.
   _____
   _____
   _____
   _____

5. What are the two places in a sentence where we find adjectives?
   _____
   _____

6. -ly words
   a. Give examples of two adverbs that end in -ly.
      (Go ahead and call your 5th grade teacher.)
      _____
      _____

# LESSON 7: USING COMMAS WITH MULTIPLE ADJECTIVES

    b. Give examples of two adjectives that end in -ly.

    _____

    _____

    c. Give examples of two adverbs that don't end in -ly.

    _____

7. What words do adjectives modify?

_____

_____

8. What words do adverbs modify?

_____

_____

9. How many questions do adverbs answer? What are the questions?

_____

_____

10. Match the following two columns:

    _____ 1. LVs    a. adjectives

    _____ 2. AcVs   b. adverbs

11. Match the following*:

    _____ 1. good   a. adverb

    _____ 2. well   b. adjective

*Don't worry about the exception.

## CHAPTER 2: THE ADJECTIVE 'MOVE' AND THE ADVERB 'MOVE'

12. When can **well** be something other than what you marked in #11?

13. Which of the following is correct under almost all circumstances?
    a. I feel good.
    b. I feel well.

Why?

14. Under what circumstances is it possible to use the other form in #13? (Notice, no one is saying this is "up for grabs grammar." If you understand the principles of grammar, it should be very clear and precise.)

15. What does "coordinate" mean?

## LESSON 7: USING COMMAS WITH MULTIPLE ADJECTIVES

16. Give me an example of two adjectives that are coordinate.

17. What does "non-coordinate" mean? Give an example of two "non-coordinate" adjectives.

18. What is the Coordinate Adjective Mastery Rule?

19. What are two tips for knowing if the adjectives are coordinate?

20. Do you remember the third tip that Kristy came up with?

CHAPTER **3**

# Punctuating Phrases

## Lesson 1: Getting Started with Phrases

Good morning, my trusty Clamdigging friends. We are about to shift gears on our road to professional Clamdiggingdom. Let me explain something to you. In the first chapter I patiently explained the difference between a **grammar piece** and its **function**. To this date we have not had to make much use of this distinction.

"Do you know why—Felix?"

"I have no idea."

"Okay, honesty is the best policy."

"Kristy? Don't know? Wow! Okay, folks, the reason is crystal clear if I show you this little diagram."

LESSON 1: GETTING STARTED WITH PHRASES

| PIECE | FUNCTION |
|:---:|:---:|
| Noun | Noun |
| Verb | Verb |
| Adjective | Adjective |
| Adverb | Adverb |

**SIMPLE GRAMMAR**

---

Not too interesting, is it? Not too useful either, as a matter of fact. But something is changing with this unit. You will NO LONGER study any grammar pieces that have the same names as their function. That last sentence is the definition of simple grammar. (Remember that and underline it for use on your final exam.) From now on we will be studying grammar that is complex (i.e. where the grammar function is not the same as the grammar piece).

In this unit you will be studying phrases in English and, more importantly, you will be learning how to punctuate phrases. (To be honest with you, punctuating the phrase is all the **Professional Clamdigger** needs, but unfortunately it is impossible to use commas with phrases if you don't know what the phrases are.) Here are the phrase 'pieces' and their functions.

---

| PHRASE PIECES | FUNCTIONS |
|:---:|:---:|
| Prepositional phrase | Adjective or Adverb |
| Participial phrase | Adjective |
| Gerund phrase | Noun |
| Appositive phrase | Adjective |

**COMPLEX GRAMMAR**

---

## CHAPTER 3: PUNCTUATING PHRASES

"Oh, no! Is this going to be on a mastery test tomorrow?"

"No, no Felix—be happy! I'm just telling you what's ahead in this whole chapter. We will take it in small steps—don't worry!"

I'm only giving it to show you that from now on that term function is going to be much more useful to us. Speaking of **terms**, let me also be sure that we are in agreement on another term that will preoccupy us quite a bit this chapter—phrase. What is a phrase?

Here's a **Professional Clamdigging**™ definition of a phrase:

A **PHRASE** is a bunch of words (two or more) that forms a grammar piece and that does NOT have both a subject *and* a verb.

(From that you can already deduce what the definition will be for a clause, can't you? Hold your horses; that's chapter 4!!)

Okay, here we go, Clamdigging fans. No, on second thought, let's take a quick quiz.

What's the definition of a phrase? (No looking back!)

Okay, the key thing for phrases is that we **don't have both a subject and a verb.**

"Today we're going to start with which phrase, G-man?"

# LESSON 1: GETTING STARTED WITH PHRASES

"I don't know, Mr. Lund."

"What do you mean, 'I don't know?' Look at the list!"

"Oh, okay—prepositional phrases?"

"Right as the rain in Spain, Giovanni. Here we go."

---

## PARTS OF THE PREPOSITIONAL PHRASE

I think you already know the basics about prepositional phrases. Here's a sentence with a prepositional phrase.

*I keep my pencils in a Snoopy cup.*

Find the prepositional phrase and underline it, please.

Yes, the prepositional phrase is **in a Snoopy cup.**

There are actually two essential parts and one optional part to a prepositional phrase. Here they are:

---

CHAPTER 3: PUNCTUATING PHRASES

---

### ESSENTIAL PARTS OF A PREPOSITIONAL PHRASE:

### 1. PREPOSITION

### 2. A NOUN OR PRONOUN (usually called the object of the preposition)

*Optional*
3. Any words **BETWEEN** the preposition and the noun

---

Please identify each of the items above in the preposition **in a Snoopy cup.**

1. *in*

2. *Snoopy cup*

3. (optional) *a*

Get it? The preposition here is **in** and the object of the preposition is **cup**. The other words (**a** and **Snoopy**) are the stuff in between—the modifiers of the phrase.

Now do the same for the prepositional phrases in the following sentences. Underline the prepositional phrase and then put a circle around the preposition and a box around the object of the preposition.

"Oops, one more thing before we look for prepositional phrases. Do you remember your prepositions? Giovanni?"

# LESSON 1: GETTING STARTED WITH PHRASES

"Let's see—you said it was position words ...'under'...'over' ...'against'?"

"Way to go, Jove! Let's do a review of prepositions."

## PREPOSITIONS

**Okay, here is a list of prepositions to remind you of some others that you may have forgotten.**

| | | | | |
|---|---|---|---|---|
| across | above | across | after | against |
| along | among | around | at | before |
| behind | below | beside(s) | between | by |
| concerning | down | during | except | for |
| from | in | into | like | of |
| off | on | over | past | since |
| through | to | up | under | until |
| with | without | within | | |

By the way, you will notice that the word preposition contains the word **position** inside of it and, indeed, prepositions often do tell us about the positions of things. Put stars* in front of the prepositions that do this. This will help you to remember the bulk of the prepositions, but don't forget about the prepositions that don't deal with locations. What is the other most common category of meaning for prepositions? Any idea, Kristy?"

"Would it be some kind of time reference? For example:
**On Tuesdays** I have a sculpture class."

"That's right—very good work. Can anyone give us another example of a time-related prepositional phrase?"

"I love to eat pancakes and bacon **in the morning**."

## CHAPTER 3: PUNCTUATING PHRASES

"Okay, now we know all about Giovanni's inner, secret, hidden life."

**Exercise 1:** Read the following sentences and do the following steps:

  A. Underline the complete prepositional phrase.
  B. Circle the preposition.
  C. Put a box around the object of the preposition
  (Warning: some sentences may have more than one prepositional phrase.)

1. We are having a Christmas party (for) the [faculty and their families].

2. Then she ripped the envelope (into) [tiny shreds].

3. Please come with us (for) a [hamburger].

4. I couldn't solve it (by) [hand], but I did solve it (with) the [calculator].

5. My best friend looks (like) [Ernest Hemingway.]

6. The student sitting (near) the [door] fell asleep just (after) the [bell rang.]

7. Every summer we visit our lake house (in) [East Texas].

8. My six year old drew all (over) the [blackboard] last night.

9. Childhood allergies often (disappear) (with) [age.]

10. I wrote the email to the principal concerning my problem (with) a [student.]

# Lesson 2: Functions of Prepositional Phrases

"Now that we know how to find a prepositional phrase, let's think about its function for a few moments. What is the function of the prepositional phrase? Okay, here we go again—you don't know, eh? You can find the function in two places.

1. _Adjectives_

2. _Adverbs_

"Do you know what they are? Kristy?"

"They function as adjectives and adverbs."

"And how the heck do you know that, Kristy."

"You told us when we started chapter 3."

"I did? Okay, wow! (Who knew that you could learn something from the teacher?) But the best place to look, in case you have forgotten, is **Mr. Lund's Magical Wheel of Function** on page 14. Check to see if you still have it. I'll be making references to it by and by.

Okay, you've got it—adjective and adverb. Now I want you to go back up to the prepositional phrases in exercise 1 and write the function—ADJ, ADV—over the phrase. But before we do that, let me ask you something important. Do you remember what questions adjectives answer? Do you remember what questions adverbs answer? Let's review these.

# CHAPTER 3: PUNCTUATING PHRASES

**ADJECTIVES**
1. Which (one)
2. What kind of
3. How many
4. How (only after a linking verb)

**ADVERBS**
1. Where
2. When
3. How
4. To what extent
5. Why* (this is a new adverb function that you will see with phrases)

**Exercise 2:** Go back to the prepositional phrases in Exercise 1 and write above it the type of phrase it is—adjective or adverb—and then write the question it answers.

1. Adverb
2. Adverb
3. Adverb
4. Adverb
5. Adjective
6. Adverb
7. Adjective
8. Adverb

LESSON 2: FUNCTIONS OF PREPOSITIONAL PHRASES

9. _Adverb_

10. _Adjective_

---

Okay, my friends, I hope you've saved your best energy for the end because **now I'm about to start teaching you the mastery material, so please pay attention**. First, a confession. I don't know exactly how to say this but the comma rule I'm about to teach you requires only that you know how to do three things:

1. Find prepositional phrases
2. Count from one to usually about two or three
3. Find the beginning of the sentence

To correctly punctuate a prepositional phrase you do NOT need to know the function of the phrase.

> "Whoa! Hold on just a minute, sir! I thought you told us that you would never ask us to know something that we didn't need for punctuation, Mr. Lund?"

"Okay, Mr. Felix. You know what? You're right! I'm sorry! My conscience has been bothering me about that. To be honest, my friend, even though the function of the phrase is not important now, it will be important later on (especially with gerunds and participles) and I thought it would be better for you to practice thinking about phrase functions with something easy like prepositional phrases rather than with the harder phrases. In any case, it'll never happen again in this course. Everything I teach you and expect you to do, you will **need** to know in order to **do** the mastery stuff. **Scout's honor!**"

Here it is: the **MASTERY RULE** and **MEMORY SENTENCE**! Put on your thinking caps, Clamdiggers!

CHAPTER 3: PUNCTUATING PHRASES

# Professional Clamdigging™ Mastery Rule:

### Prepositional Phrase Comma Rule

Whenever you have two or more prepositional phrases at the beginning of the sentence, set them off with a COMMA.

## Professional Clamdigging™ Memory Sentence

**Prepositional Phrase Comma Rule**

In my room under my bed, you'll find my geometry textbook.

## LESSON 2: FUNCTIONS OF PREPOSITIONAL PHRASES

If those two conditions are not met, **NO COMMA**!!! **Period. Ever!** (By the way, this is the first example of the introducer comma rule. The professional clamdigger will notice and remember that there is a **HOST** of grammar 'pieces' that require a comma **ONLY** if they appear at the beginning of the sentence. In other words, if you can recognize that piece and can find the beginning of the sentence, you will be an instant master of a huge number of comma applications. By applying that rule alone, you will be able to dazzle everyone you come in contact with—your mom, the love of your life, your secretary, the President of the United States... More on that later.)

Comma needed:

 1                  2
**In my room under my bed**, you'll find my geometry textbook.

No comma needed:

You'll find my geometry textbook **in my room under the bed.**

Notice: we have the same prepositional phrases but they are not at the beginning of the sentence, so there is NO COMMA!

**Exercise 3**: Look at the following sentences. If a comma is required, **put C** in front of the sentence, and then put in the comma and **circle the comma**. If no comma is required, **put an NC** in front of the sentence.

C 1. After the game, we're going to Quickie Burger.

NC 2. I haven't seen her since 2009.

C 3. I left your key, under the front tire of your car.

## CHAPTER 3: PUNCTUATING PHRASES

4. After his meeting with Miss Klekamp, he's going back to his office.

5. In the cupboard, on the third shelf, you'll find the napkins.

6. After the change in time, I'm always late for church.

7. Underneath the stones, by that tree, are some strange fragments of pottery.

8. Behind the blue jar, on the top shelf, I keep my piggy bank.

9. Down the hall, to the left, are the restrooms.

10. In the morning, for our meeting, let's go to Crossroads in Dallas.

---

### PREPOSITIONAL PHRASE COMMA RULE EXCEPTION

Oooooooooooooooooooooops, I forget to tell you one other thing: one and only one wonderful exception to this rule—but not too unusual to appear on mastery exams.

> **Exception:** In some cases involving the verb BE (hint, hint!) the positions of the subject and verb are reversed (first, last; last, first). In this case there is NO comma.
>
>                                                              **V**        **Subj**
> **Example**: Inside my purse at the end of the table **is** your car **key**.

Do you see how the verb comes before the subject here? This can only happen, by the way, when prepositional phrases come at the beginning of the sentence.

However, if we put a subject in its usual position before the verb without changing the number or position of the prepositional phrases, the rule functions as usual.

## LESSON 2: FUNCTIONS OF PREPOSITIONAL PHRASES

        **Prep Phrases**        **Subject**
Inside my purse **at** the end of the table, **she** found my car key.

So be sure that there is a subject at the end of the prepositional phrases that you are working so hard to locate and count. And remember, in commands the subject is 'understood' but it is definitely there.

        **You**
After your meeting with Dr. Rayburn, call me right away.

Check now to see if there are any exceptions to the prepositional phrase comma rule in Exercise 3. If so, put a big * in front of that number.

CHAPTER 3: PUNCTUATING PHRASES

# Lesson 3: *The Black Hole:* Objective Forms of the Pronoun (me, them, him, her)

"My dear reader, there is one last item that is standing between you and I* and the end of the section. Do you know what it is? While you're thinking about that, go back and find the error in the last sentence. What is the error?"

"'Between you and I' is wrong; it should be 'between you and me.'"

"Yes, Kristy! That's right. I'm going to have you transferred into Dr. Prausnitz' seminar: The Black Holes of Grammar. **You and I** should be **you and me**. Why? Because <u>me</u> is the object form of the first person singular subject pronoun (I/me). And inside a prepositional phrase (The wall fell on Joe) the pronoun must be in the object (or objective) form."

---

### Objective Forms of the Pronoun (me, them, him, her)

This is not nearly as difficult as it sounds. Let's take a good look at this.

Is the following sentence correct, Felix? Please say no!"

**The wall fell on I*.**

"No!"

"Okay, then—how would you say it."

**"The wall fell on me."**

142

# LESSON 3: THE BLACK HOLE: OBJECTIVE FORMS OF THE PRONOUN (ME, THEM, HIM, HER)

Very good, Mr. Happiness! Even Amateur Clamdiggers know this. And you are way beyond amateurs by now.

Would you say the wall fell on she? (Write the correct form.)

How about this? The wall fell on he. (Fix it, please)

The wall fell on they? (This is the last time.)

Okay, good. You have now made a good list of the objective pronouns in English. Here's a list of them all.

---

## PERSONAL PRONOUNS

| SUBJECTIVE FORM | OBJECTIVE FORM |
| --- | --- |
| I | Me |
| We | Us |
| She | Her |
| He | Him |
| They | Them |
| You | You* |

---

*Notice the second person pronoun <u>you</u> is the same in both the subject(ive) and object(ive) forms, so I'm not going to bother you with that.

Now, the place where Amateur Clamdiggers and almost everybody else gets confused is when there are two people in the prepositional phrase. You see?

There is a black beetle sitting between you and **(I/me).**

# CHAPTER 3: PUNCTUATING PHRASES

**Circle the correct word. Use the information from above.**
Did you use the objective pronoun?

**Exercise 4**: Choose the correct form of the pronouns in the following sentences.

_____ 1. There is a brown beetle sitting between Phil and (she/**her**).

_____ 2. There is a scary spider sitting between (she/**her**) and (he/**him**).

_____ 3. Giovanni is going to the farmers market on Saturday with Trisha and (I/**me**).

_____ 4. The boat slammed over John's uncle and (I/**me**).

_____ 5. Who's going with Sue and (I/**me**)?

_____ 6. Are you playing tennis today with Alisha and (he/**him**)?

---

Probably the one that most people get wrong (and I mean educated people here, folks) is putting in the 'I' form when it should be the 'me' form. Maybe that's because we had teachers who wanted us to be polite and put the other person first: "Johnny, say Alex and I, not me and Alex." Well, as a result, not too many of us say "me and Alex" anymore, but I guarantee you a lot of us are not sure whether to use 'I' or 'me' in a sentence.

LESSON 3: THE BLACK HOLE: OBJECTIVE FORMS OF THE PRONOUN (ME, THEM, HIM, HER)

# Professional Clamdigging™ Mastery Rule:

## Subject/Object Pronoun Mastery Rule

If a pronoun is in the subject part of the sentence, use the subjective form (I, he, they). If the pronoun is in the object (or predicate) part of the sentence, OR, if it is in a prepositional phrase anywhere in the sentence, use the objective form (me, him, her, them).

## Professional Clamdigging™ Memory Sentence

**Subject/Object Pronoun Memory Sentence**

1. Joe and I are working late tonight. (subject part)
2. He gave the late shift to Joe and me. (object part)
3. Nobody's working tonight with Joe and me. (object of prepositional phrase.)

# CHAPTER 3: PUNCTUATING PHRASES

**Exercise 5**: Circle the correct pronoun in the following sentences. Review the "I/Me Rule" before you begin.

1. Are you giving both assignments to Jill and (I/**me**)?

2. Ryan and (**I**/me) can't leave until Tuesday.

3. Did Stephanie see you and (I/**me**) at the dance?

4. Your uncle and (**she**/her) got locked out of the house.

5. The Irving Fire Department and (**we**/us) are having a picnic on the 14th of August.

6. Did you and (**he**/him) order the pizzas?

7. Between you and (**I**/me), I'm actually starting to get this.

8. I can't believe her mother won't trust her to go out with you and (I/**me**).

9. Jill is that one on the right, standing behind Jack and (I/**me**).

10. Don and (**I**/me) will be waiting for you on Forest and Stults.

So long, sports fans! Get some serious sleep, Felix. Tomorrow we start **participial phrases**, and no, you're not developing a tummy ache—not a tooth ache either.

# Lesson 4: Participial Phrases: DUM, Da DUM DUM!

"Okay, now that you have prepositional phrases under your belt, **it's time to move on to uh .... uh**."

"No. No. Please, not that! ANYTHING BUT THAT!"

"Come on now, Felix; you're usually a really upbeat, happy guy. Be reasonable. Please get control of yourself. And please stop banging your head against the desk; I can't concentrate with all that racket. How do you expect me to think?"

"But, but…you said…"

There, there. That's better. Calm down. Take some deep breaths, Felix baby. There. Okay. Good. (G e n t l e W h i s p e r): Participial Phrases.

See it's out now. There it is. That wasn't so bad, was it? I said it as gently as I could. Now the worst is over. Let's take it nice and slowly. While I think of an example or two, why don't you go to the *Mr. Lund's Magical Wheel of Function* (page 14) and see what the participial phrase does anyway.

"And the answer, Mr. Giovanni, is?"

"It tells more about nouns."

"Exactamundo."

Okay, let's look at an example. Here's a **participial phrase**. (The participial phrase is bolded).

## CHAPTER 3: PUNCTUATING PHRASES

>**Insulted by the tone of his voice,** she hit the end button on her cell phone.

What word does the participial phrase modify? What should it modify? Remember what it said on the *Magical Wheel of Function*? Yes, it should modify a noun. Draw an arrow to the word that **insulted by the tone of his voice** is modifying.

Your arrow should point to **she**. Did you get that right, Giovanni?

> "That really doesn't make any sense, Mr. Lund."

Well, I know. It does sound a little strange. Let me try to help you with this. To get it to make sense, let's put it this way: which 'she' are we speaking of in this sentence? The 'she' that was **insulted by the tone of his voice**, or, if you prefer, the *"insulted-by-the-tone-of-his-voice"* '**she.**' It does sound weird, but that is really close to the way our English-speaking brains process that information deep down.

By the way, I know that I told you that with prepositional phrases knowing the function was not absolutely essential for you to punctuate correctly, but with the participial phrase it is very important. Why? Because in our next lesson I'm going to introduce you to *gerunds and gerunds look exactly like -ing participles* (like in #2) and the only way to tell the difference and to know when to use or NOT use commas is by the FUNCTION of the phrase. So look sharp and don't take any commercial breaks here.

"So, let me ask one more time: what function do participial phrases have, Kristy?"

> "The Adjective function."

"Very good, my friend. And what words do they modify, Felix?"

> "Nouns and pronouns."

## LESSON 4: PARTICIPIAL PHRASES: DUM, DA DUM DUM!

"Bravo. That's my man!"

"This all seems like a lot of trouble, Mr. Lund. What's the point of all this? What if I promise never to use one of these participial phrases? Can I skip this mastery rule?"

No way, Felix! Look at what you'd be missing. A **participial phrase** is really quite cool and amazing. It lets you talk about two things happening at one time. Look at this:

*She was smiling like a Cheshire Cat.*
She slammed the door in my face.

*Smiling like a Cheshire Cat,* she slammed the door in my face.

Neat, eh? You pack more action into your sentence, and not only is it fun for you, but it's fun for your reader too. It's a little like watching two TV screens at the same time.

Okay, now how do we punctuate participial phrases? Here are the memory sentences and the mastery rule for the two participial phrases:

## CHAPTER 3: PUNCTUATING PHRASES

### Professional Clamdigging™ Memory Sentence
**Past Participial Phrase**

**Insulted by the tone of his voice,** she hit the end button on her cell phone.

### Professional Clamdigging™ Memory Sentence
**Present Participial Phrase**

**Smiling like a Cheshire cat,** she slammed the door in my face.

LESSON 4: PARTICIPIAL PHRASES: DUM, DA DUM DUM!

# Professional Clamdigging™ Mastery Rule:

## Participial Phrase Comma Rule

### Set off with commas any participial phrase in a sentence.

Do you know what this means—setting off a phrase with commas? Let me show you. In some cases you use one comma and in other cases you use two commas. It depends on the position of the participial phrase. Here are all the possibilities:

Let me show you how this works:

**Grabbing his lunch**, Mr. Lund stumbled his way to the front door. (one comma)

Mr. Lund, **grabbing his lunch**, stumbled his way to the front door. (two commas)

Mr. Lund stumbled to the door, **grabbing his lunch on the way**. (one comma)

# CHAPTER 3: PUNCTUATING PHRASES

**Exercise 6**: Underline the participial phrase in the following sentences; then set off the phrase with commas.

1. <u>Exhausted by the heat</u>, she fainted and fell into the rose bushes.

2. <u>Speeding away from the police</u>, the Amateur Clamdigger got stuck in a large sand dune.

3. <u>Watching the silver drop of sweat trickle down the neck of the man in front of me</u>, I took another step forward in the line at the entrance to Six Flags.

4. The Russian General, <u>mortally wounded</u>, lay face down on the billiards table.

5. <u>Turning from his video game</u>, my older brother patiently explained the concept of participial phrases.

6. I finished reading all the *Macbeth* papers, <u>working well into the night</u>.

7. <u>Burnt to a crisp from the sun</u>, I ran for shade.

8. Michael Jordan, <u>flying through the air</u>, slammed the ball through the hoop.

9. Hans walked into the room, <u>waving his hands violently</u>.

10. <u>Turning the corner too fast</u>, she slipped and fell on her face.

11. The Achaeans, <u>marching silently</u>, fell upon the Trojans like lions.

Check your answers.

### LESSON 4: PARTICIPIAL PHRASES: DUM, DA DUM DUM!

### AVOIDING A DANGLING ---\
                                                         /
                                                         \
                                                         /
###                                    MODIFIER

By the way, let me take a minute and show you something that gives English teachers lots of laughs. It's called a 'dangling modifier.' (Sorry to get technical on you.)

**Professional Clamdigging Tip**

When you start a sentence with a participial phrase, **always put the subject of the sentence after the participial phrase.**

"Now for some laughs. What's the subject in this sentence, Kristy?"

*Running to my locker, a banana got stuck on my foot, and I slipped and fell on my butt.*

    "A banana."

"Can you tell me what that sentence above is really saying, Kristy?"

    "It's saying that the banana was running to my locker and got stuck under my feet and I fell on my butt."

"Funny stuff, eh? Got the picture? The banana is the subject of the sentence, so the banana is doing all the work—huffing and puffing and tripping up the poor student named Kristy. Pretty idiotic, isn't it? So unless you want to end up on your English teachers list of 'Funny

153

CHAPTER 3: PUNCTUATING PHRASES

things that students wrote today,'

---

**REMEMBER**:
Make sure to put the subject **right after the participial phrase**
if it is at the beginning of the sentence.

---

"Can you fix that one, Kristy?"

"Running to my locker, I slipped on a banana and fell on my butt."

"That's much better. Thank you."

Let's try to correct a few of these dangling modifiers.

**Exercise 7**: Look at these sentences with dangling modifiers and try to find what is funny or ridiculous in each and then correct it by putting the correct subject after the participial phrase. If a comma is required, put it in the sentence and circle it.

1. Turning east on Flora Street, the Symphony Hall sparkled.

2. Driving around a curve at 60 miles an hour, the elk stood like a wall in the middle of the road.

## LESSON 4: PARTICIPIAL PHRASES: DUM, DA DUM DUM!

3. Having vacuumed the dining room and set the table, the house was ready for the dinner party with the Cousers.

   _____

4. Walking home from school, his backpack strap broke and crashed on the sidewalk.

   _____

---

"It looks like we're all done with this lesson, Clamdiggers. That wasn't so bad, was it, Felix? I'll take that silence as a no. Tomorrow we have one more little problem to solve before we say goodbye to participles."

CHAPTER 3: PUNCTUATING PHRASES

# Lesson 5: Generating Past Participial Phrases

Okay folks, let's review the memory sentences that we know so far. You'll need to write out these sentences perfectly before I let you take the next unit test, so you want to be sure that you know them cold. Say them out loud and—most important—If there is a comma in the sentence, say "COMMA" when you come to the place where the comma should be.

You memorize: Smiling like a Cheshire Cat, she slammed the door in my face.

You SAY: Smiling like a Cheshire Cat (,COMMA) she slammed the door in my face.

Got it? Here are your memory sentences so far:

**Memory Sentences:**

**Prepositional phrase**: In my room under my bed, you'll find my geometry textbook.

**Past participial phrase**: Insulted by the tone of his voice, she hit the end button on the cell phone.

**Present participial phrase:** Smiling like a Cheshire Cat, she slammed the door in my face.

Be sure to **memorize** these memory sentences before class tomorrow.

By the way, do you know the difference between the present and past participial phrase? It's not really that hard. Let me show you—no extra charge.

A **past participial phrase** begins with a **past participle**; a **present participial** phrase begins with a **present participle**.

## LESSON 5: GENERATING PAST PARTICIPIAL PHRASES

"Great. Thanks, Mr. Lund. Now do you mind telling us how to make present and past participles?"

"Certainly, Felix. For you that will be my pleasure. By the way, do I detect the dark clouds of sarcasm sliding into your blue sky?"

Okay, Clamdiggers—let's go to work on past participles. Here's a quick way to determine the past participle form of any verb.

---

**Past** participle maker
**(kind of tricky)**:

She has _____ a lot.
(studied, fallen, run etc.)

---

And here's a cheap, quick way to find the **present participle** of a **verb**.

---

**Present** participle maker
**(very easy!)**:

She has been _____ a lot.
(studying, falling, running, etc.)

---

(So for the present participle, all you're doing is taking a verb in its simple form and adding -ing.)

I tell you what: let's try to make some participles. This is going to be fun! Let's do a couple together and then I'll let you do the rest on your own.

# CHAPTER 3: PUNCTUATING PHRASES

"Giovanni, what's the **past participle** form of the verb 'begin'? And please use the **past participle maker**, if you don't mind? Go ahead and put in extra words so it makes as much sense as possible."

"She has begun new diet plans many times."

"Okay, good. Felix, you do the **present participle** of the same verb."

"She has been beginning new diet plans for years."

"Okay, Kristy, do the **past participle** of 'know.'"

"She has known a lot of good fortune in her life."

"Good. That's what I call a happy sentence. And Felix. You do the **present participle** form of that verb."

"She has been knowing a lot of secrets about Mr. Lund."

"Trying to put me on the defensive, eh? All right, good job. Do the rest of these on your own. Good luck!"

**Exercise 8:** For each of the following verbs, please write out the past participle form and the present participle form.

| Verb | Past Participle | Present Participle |
| --- | --- | --- |
| 1. see | seen | seeing |
| 2. draw | drawn | drawing |

LESSON 5: GENERATING PAST PARTICIPIAL PHRASES

| 3. steal | stolen | stealing |
| 4. say | said | saying |
| 5. leave | left | leaving |
| 6. spit | spit | spitting |
| 7. strike | struck | striking |
| 8. slam | slammed | slamming |
| 9. master | mastered | mastering |
| 10. take | taken | taking |

**Exercise 9**: Let's try to punctuate a few sentences. First underline any phrases that you see in the following sentences. Also, write the type of phrase (prep, past part., present part.) over the phrase. Then put in the comma and circle the comma and put "C" in front of the sentence, or if no comma is necessary, put "NC" in front of the sentence.

C 1. Standing on the chairs, we watched the approaching storm clouds. — Present

NC 2. I'll meet you on the corner in front of Denny's. — Prep

NC 3. Bubba entered the room, pushing everyone out of his way. — Present

## CHAPTER 3: PUNCTUATING PHRASES

C 4. Surrounded by loving teammates, she burst into tears.
         Past

C 5. On the first Thursday of the month, we have our class meetings.
              Prep

C 6. Lunging for the ball, I fell into a crowd of surprised parents.
              Present

NC 7. In the corner of my closet are my favorite running shoes.
              Prep

C 8. Trapped by the incoming tide, Pete tweeted desperately for help.
              Past

C 9. The two brothers, caught in the downpour, waited under the bridge, for the storm to pass.
              Past and Prep

C 10. The Rangers pitcher retired the sides, striking out the last two batters.
              Present

---

Check your answers tomorrow in class, please.

# Lesson 6: The Gerund Phrase

Now we're ready for the next phrase. And you're going to want to buy the t-shirt of this one! Do you see a phrase in this sentence, Giovanni?

  Running across LBJ* is not a smart idea.
     *A very busy expressway/tollway in Dallas, Texas.

  "I think so. Isn't Running across LBJ a phrase?"

"What is a phrase again? Kristy?

  "A bunch of words that forms a grammar piece, right?"

"Good. Is it a prepositional phrase, Kristy?"

  "No, there is no preposition."

"No preposition anywhere in sight. How about a participial phrase?"

  "Yeah, it looks like a like a participial phrase, but I don't think it is one."

"That's my Kristy. What's the memory sentence for the present participial phrase?"

  *"Smiling like a Cheshire Cat, (comma!) she . . . ."*

Okay, let's hit the pause button right there—sorry to freeze frame you, Kristy. So it looks like a present participial phrase, but **IS IT** a present participial phrase? Let's test this sentence against a sentence that we know is a participial phrase.

## CHAPTER 3: PUNCTUATING PHRASES

### PRESENT PARTICIPLE PHRASE:

1. **Smiling like a Cheshire Cat,** she slammed the door in his face.

### MYSTERY PHRASE:

2. **Running across LBJ** is not a smart idea.

Now I'm going to take you step by step through a process of thinking about the participial phrase and the 'mystery' phrase. If you want to be a Professional Clamdigger, you must learn this process of thinking. The process is as important as the answer. So pay attention and reread the next three paragraphs as many times as you need to in order to fully understand this process.

### For Finding Gerunds

"What function does the participial phrase piece perform, Felix?"

"The adjective function."

"Good. So that means that it modifies what kind of word, Giovanni?"

"A noun."

"Now look at the phrase in sentence 1. What is it again, Giovanni?"

# LESSON 6: THE GERUND PHRASE

"Smiling like a Cheshire Cat."

"Is it modifying a noun? A subject maybe?"

"Yes, it's modifying 'she.'"

"That's right. And 'she' is a noun and so the phrase is a present participial phrase. Now, let's look at sentence 2. What's the phrase in this case, Giovanni?"

"'Running across LBJ.'"

"Okay, and is it modifying the subject?"

"Tell you the truth, Mr. Lund—I don't even know what the subject is."

"What is the verb?"

"It's 'is.' But what's the subject? It can't be 'running,' can it?"

"Everybody sit down and take some deep breaths. This may come as a shock, but the truth is that the subject is '**running across LBJ**.' Felix?"

"'**Running across LBJ**' is the subject? It looks like a verb to me."

Yeah, it does, but the verb is 'is.' We know that. So if 'is' is the verb, then 'running' can't be the verb. That's the kind of thinking that you need to do to grasp this. **Very clear, logical thinking**. The **gerund** is known as a **verbal**, which means that it looks and sounds and acts like a verb, but it's not a verb. It's a noun. Or to give its proper name, it is a **gerund**. So the **gerund phrase** is 'Running across LBJ.'

# CHAPTER 3: PUNCTUATING PHRASES

Let's figure out how to cook up one of these gerund phrases. We'll start with the gerund. To make a gerund follow this recipe:

1. Take one English verb.

2. Add -ing to the end of the verb.

That's it and you have a gerund. As you can see, other words like modifiers (**running fast**) or prepositions (**running like a madman**) will often go with the gerund, forming a gerund phrase.

"Now let me ask you a question. If a gerund phrase can be a subject, what function does it have? Make an educated guess and then look at the *Mr. Lund's Magical Wheel of Function* on page 14, and then I'll meet you back here. Felix, you're up to bat!"

"Is it a noun?"

"It's a noun—right as rain, buddy! Now if a gerund can be a subject, can it be located anywhere else in the sentence? Yes, you will see gerunds in any part of the sentence just like you see nouns in any part of the sentence. What grammar pieces do the noun function, Kristy?"

"Uh, **nouns** can be subjects, objects, or objects of prepositions."

"Good job, Kristy. Here are some examples of gerunds in each of these positions."

1. **Running across LBJ** is not a smart idea. (subject)

2. My dopey friend Alex loves **skate-boarding across LBJ**. (direct object)

3. Pat is very good **at lying through his teeth**. (object of the preposition)

## LESSON 6: THE GERUND PHRASE

Now, since gerund phrases can be found anywhere in the sentence and they look just like present participles (or seem to), they might be hard to find. Here's a tip that might help you. If you see a phrase beginning with an -ing word, try to do the following.

*Professional Clamdigging* **Tip**

### The Gerund Phrase Test

### 1. Underline
Underline the -ing word and modifiers
(the other words that come right after the gerund).

### 2. Try to take out this phrase and replace it with "WHAT"
If the sentence makes sense with the word **what**, then you have a real-life, true-blue gerund phrase. If it doesn't make sense, chances are you have a participial phrase.

Let's try this out to see if it works. Try these tips for the three gerund phrase examples above. And tell me if the sentence makes sense with the test word.

"Kristy, will you do the honors for the first one, please?"

"(What) is not a good idea. Yeah, that makes sense, Mr. Lund."

"G-man, please do number two."

# CHAPTER 3: PUNCTUATING PHRASES

"My goofy friend Alex likes (what)."

"Does that work?"

"Yup!"

"Felix, number three is all yours."

"Joe is good at (what)."

Got it? Okay, each of these phrases can be replaced by 'what,' so that means that they are all **gerund phrases**. Does it work on our *participial phrase memory phrase*, Kristy?"

"Nope. (What) she closed the door in my face."

"Ha ha ha ha ha ha ha ha!"

"Okay, Mr. Lund. It's really not that funny."

"So we just proved that that sentence is not a gerund, so it must be a what, Kristy?"

"A present participial phrase."

Now practice the **gerund phrase test** on these sentences in Exercise 10.

**LESSON 6: THE GERUND PHRASE**

**Exercise 10**: Put **G** in front of the sentence if it contains a gerund phrase, and put **NO** if it doesn't.

G 1. I am not in favor of electing him to the Senate.

NO 2. Placing his books on the table, he sat down and fell asleep.

G 3. Standing up for your rights is a mark of a healthy person.

NO 4. Aiming carefully, she pulled the trigger and hit the target.

G 5. Concentrating carefully is the key to winning at chess.

---

Now you're probably wondering, WHAT IS THE GERUND PHRASE MASTERY RULE, right? Ahem. Finally, I have some good news for youse. (That's Chicago English!)

# Professional Clamdigging™ Mastery Rule:

## Gerund Phrase Comma Rule

There are NO commas with gerund phrases.

### CHAPTER 3: PUNCTUATING PHRASES

Not bad, eh? It makes also sense when you think about it like a Professional Clamdigger. You wouldn't put a comma between a subject and a verb, would you?

**WRONG:** *John, is late. Ha ha ha ha ha!

**RIGHT:** John is late. Yes, right.

Same with gerunds:

Running across LBJ is not a smart idea.

Oh, by the way, here is the memory sentence that Felix has been waiting for (somewhat patiently, I should add).

*Professional Clamdigging*™
*Memory Sentence*
**Gerund Phrase**

**Running across LBJ*** is not a smart idea.
* A very busy expressway/tollway in Dallas.

By the way, if you're still having trouble distinguishing between a present (-ing) participial phrase and a gerund phrase, here's another tip:

**LESSON 6: THE GERUND PHRASE**

### Professional Clamdigging Tip

A participial phrase can be moved around in the sentence without destroying the sentence. A gerund cannot.

**Pulling up on the reins, Ben Cartwright motioned for us to stop our horse.**

**Ben Cartwright, pulling up on the reins, motioned for us to stop.**

Now try to do this with your gerund memory sentence. Got it?

**Exercise 11:** This exercise will mix up prepositional phrases, past and present participial phrases, and gerund phrases. Underline the phrase and write above it what kind of phrase it is. Then put in any commas that are necessary and circle the commas. If no comma is necessary, put NC in front of the sentence.

__NC__ 1. Studying for a Mastery English test [G] is not one of my favorite things to do.

__C__ 2. Studying for the Mastery English test [Present], she fell asleep and bumped her head on the desk.

__C__ 3. After the game on Tuesday [Prep], I'm leaving for Padre Island.

__C__ 4. She ran into the room, clinging to her purse and books [Present].

__NC__ 5. Beside the lamp on the bureau [Prep] are your car keys.

# CHAPTER 3: PUNCTUATING PHRASES

__NC__ 6. <u>Saying goodbye</u> is really hard for me. [G above "goodbye"]

__C__ 7. <u>On the first day of the month,</u> we have Student Council meetings. [Prep]

__C__ 8. <u>Circling the airport to wait for landing instructions,</u> our plane encountered some rough weather. [Present]

__NC__ 9. <u>After the dance</u> they're coming to our house. [Prep]

__C__ 10. <u>Feeling a metallic crunch,</u> my body was whipped against the steering wheel. [Present]

__C__ 11. <u>Talking to my parents on the phone,</u> I had a strange feeling that I was there with them. [Present]

__NC__ 12. <u>Forgiving other people</u> is hard for him. [G]

__C__ 13. <u>Smiling like a Cheshire Cat,</u> he closed the door in my face. [Present]

---

Check your answers and be happy!

# Lesson 7: The Appositive Phrase

Before we go any further, write down your *memory sentences* for the following phrases:

Introductory prepositional phrases:
_____

Past participial phrase:
_____

Present participial phrase:
_____

Gerund phrase:
_____

### Professional Clamdigging Tip

**Tip for Memory Sentences:**

Make up a card (like your vocabulary cards) and put the grammar piece (gerund phrase) on one side and put the memory sentence on the other.

These memory sentences will be on the mastery exam. That means you must write down the memory sentences to achieve mastery from now on.

"But why do we have to memorize all these sentences?"

## CHAPTER 3: PUNCTUATING PHRASES

"Felix, the difference between you Clamdiggers and everybody else out there is that most people forget the grammar item right after they finish the exam. But not Professional Clamdiggers. Clamdiggers know that they will have mastery exams on the memory sentences all the way to the end of the course. So, when you Clamdiggers memorize something, you will have the item locked inside you, and you will be able to compare your memory sentences with other new sentences that you encounter out there in your work and studies. Then you will know whether to punctuate them or not. **That's the magic of memory sentences and mastery.**

Let's move on to our last important phrase piece. Here are three examples of the appositive phrase. The first one is your *memory sentence*.

*Professional Clamdigging*™
*Memory Sentence*
Appositive Phrase

Mr. Lund, **my Clamdigging teacher,** comes from Chicago.

Salsa, **MY FAVORITE DANCE MUSIC**, is very popular in the Carribean.

My son's car, **A 1997 CAMRY**, needs a new engine.

"Okay, now let me ask you some questions about these phrases, Kristy. Where can the appositive phrase be found in the sentence?"

"It looks like it comes after the subject or the noun."

LESSON 7: THE APPOSITIVE PHRASE

"What is its function?"

"I think that it is restating the subject—giving more information about the subject."

---

**APPOSITIVE PHRASES**
are really quite simple.
What they do is simple: they restate what a noun is.

| **SUBJECT** | **APPOSITIVE** |
|---|---|
| Joe Richards, | the funniest guy in our English class |
| My truck, | a 2008 Nissan |

---

Do you see what the appositive phrases are saying?

Joe Richards = the funniest guy in our English class.

My truck = a 2008 Nissan.

"Yes, Kristy?"

"It looks to me like the appositive phrase can be converted into a predicate noun following a linking verb."

**Joe Richards** is **the funniest guy** in our English class.

My **truck** is a 2008 **Nissan.**

That's exactly right. But notice Kristy's sentences only allow us to say one thing about Joe Richards and my truck. With an appositive phrase we can say two things about each of these subjects.

## CHAPTER 3: PUNCTUATING PHRASES

                    **#1**                                        **#2**

Joe Richards, the funniest guy in my English class, wants to go out with my girlfriend.

             **#1**         **#2**

My truck, a 2008 Nissan, loves ice storms.

Got it? More power for a sentence. Do you remember the other piece we've studied that allowed you to say two things about a subject? Write out the memory sentence for this… something about **smiling**—remember? And being **insulted**?

"Giovanni?"

    "Smiling like a Cheshire cat, she slammed the door in my face."

"Perfectomundo—the present participial phrase. And what are the two things that we are saying about the subject?"

    "She's smiling and she slammed the door in my face. She must be mad at me."

"Great and uh…Felix, do you know the other one?"

    "Insulted by the tone of his voice, she hit the end button on her cell phone. She was insulted and she hung up on him."

"Very good. Now one last thing. Where do we find these **appositives**? Giovanni?"

    "If they come after a noun, then they can be after the subject or object or the object of the preposition."

Very good. Let's look at examples of each of these three positions.

## LESSON 7: THE APPOSITIVE PHRASE

Mr. Lund, **my Clamdigging teacher,** **comes from Chicago**. (after the subject)

She gave the essay to Mr. Lund, **my Clamdigging teacher.** (after the object)

My cousin lives in Austin, **the capital of Texas.** (after the object of the preposition)

Thanks. In other words—which Mr. Lund? The Mr. Lund that is my Clamdigging teacher. How do you recognize an appositive phrase? To be sure you have an appositive phrase, look for the noun at the end of the phrase (see below):

### Professional Clamdigging Tip

Notice that the appositive restates or renames the noun and there may be several words in the appositive, but the last word is always a noun.

**Noun**          **Noun**
Mr. Lund, **my Clamdigging teacher,** comes from Chicago. (after the subject)

              **Noun**          **Noun**
She gave the essay to Mr. Lund, **my Clamdigging teacher.** (after the object)

CHAPTER 3: PUNCTUATING PHRASES

      **Noun**   **Noun**
**My cousin lives in Austin, the capital of Texas. (after the object of the preposition)**

Okay, Clamdiggers—here's the mastery rule for the appositives.

# Professional Clamdigging™ Mastery Rule:

### Appositive Phrase Mastery Rule

**Set off all appositive phrases with commas.**

**Exercise 12**: Put commas in the following sentence if there are appositive phrases and circle your commas. If there is no appositive phrase, write NC in front of the sentence.

 C 1. I gave the schedules to Mrs. Betten, his advisor.

 C 2. Dallas Lutheran School, a private Christian school, is located on Stults Road.

 C 3. Dr. Prausnitz, my favorite English teacher, was born in Germany.

## LESSON 7: THE APPOSITIVE PHRASE

_C_  4. I gave the tax documents to Terri Petrick, my son's new boss.

_C_  5. Mrs. Aurich, our former secretary, is the most patient human being alive.

_C_  6. We'll have our next meeting on October 12th, the second Wednesday of the month.

_C_  7. We're meeting at the gym on the 22nd, the fourth Thursday in August.

---

Check with the boss for answers and get some rest!

CHAPTER 3: PUNCTUATING PHRASES

# Lesson 8: The Infinitive Phrase

"You know what—I've been bothered all night about something."

"Is your dog sick?"

"No, Felix, my dog isn't sick, but if I had one, I would thank you for asking."

"I can tell that you haven't been sleeping well—you have bags under your eyes."

"Well, thank you, Kristy, for that wonderful piece of information."

"Let's hear it, Mr. Lund: what's bothering you? You know you want to tell us."

"All right, let me get this off my chest. I think I told you that there was another kind of phrase—**The Infinitive Phrase**, but that I wasn't going to teach it to you because it wasn't worth the trouble and now the infinitive clause fairy is bugging me day and night, so how about I just show you one, okay? After all, who wants to leave the zoo without seeing the hippo, even though that graceful creature with the dazzling, toothy grin is not one of my favorite animals?"

"Here we go. How many of you have studied Spanish? By the way, I used to teach Spanish. Me llamaba Sr. Chavo."

"Whoa, wait a minute—let's speak English here, please, can we, Mr. Lund? What did you just say?"

"He said: my Spanish name used to be Mr. Chavo."

"Thank you, Mr. Giovanni. You know something—you've got class. Somebody should write an opera and name it after you."

## LESSON 8: THE INFINITIVE PHRASE

"As I was saying before I was so rudely interrupted—if you have studied Spanish, infinitive phrases will be very easy for you because all Spanish verbs start out in the form of the infinitive—like 'hablar' and 'comer' and 'vivir'—which mean 'to speak' and 'to eat' and 'to live.'

So if a phrase begins with 'to' and then a verb, you know that you have an infinitive phrase. Ready for the memory sentence and the mastery rule?

### Professional Clamdigging™ Memory Sentence
**Infinitive Phrase**

**To punctuate correctly,** you need to know a little grammar.

### Professional Clamdigging™ Mastery Rule:

**Infinitive Phrase Comma Rule**

Set off with a comma any infinitive phrase at the beginning of a sentence.

CHAPTER 3: PUNCTUATING PHRASES

**Exception: DO <u>NOT</u> PUT A COMMA AFTER AN INFINITIVE PHRASE THAT IS FOLLOWED BY A VERB.** Notice this is really the same as the exception to the prepositional phrase rule (In my room under my bed is my geometry textbook) and the gerund phrase rule (Running across LBJ is not a smart idea).

      **Infinitive phrase  Verb**
Example:  <u>To be or not to be</u> **is** the question.  (no comma)

**Exercise 13**: Put commas in the following sentences as necessary. Circle the comma to be sure that it is very clear.

1. To become a doctor, you will need to start with an undergraduate degree.

2. I was hoping to call you later this afternoon.

3. To create a sense of excitement in the publishing world, you need to get the media on-board.

4. I wanted to go for a swim this afternoon, but ran out of time.

5. To take a new stance is often difficult.

6. To make bread, you need flour and yeast and milk and sugar and a few other ingredients.

7. To succeed in the computer field it helps to know a lot of math.

8. To really help someone, you need to try to understand the world from her point of view.

180

LESSON 8: THE INFINITIVE PHRASE

"Okay, here are some tips for keeping up with all of these phrases—and get ready because coming up next is an exercise that mixes them all together—your worst nightmare, Felix."

(Woeful silence.)

"Just kidding, buddy—you'll do fine! Check this out!"

### FOR PUNCTUATING PHRASES:

**1a. Look for -ing words ('looking,' 'running').** These are often in the beginning of the sentence. Underline the whole phrase. **If the phrase is followed by a SUBJECT, then it is a participial phrase. Set it off with commas.**

S

Running like a maniac, she crashed into Mr. Greimann.

**If the phrase is followed by a verb, it is a gerund phrase and does not require commas.**

V

Running like a maniac is not a good way to impress your boyfriend.

**1b. Look for past participial phrases that may need to be set off with commas.**

# CHAPTER 3: PUNCTUATING PHRASES

## 2. Look for appositive phrases

Write in your memory phrase as an example:

*To punctuate correctly you need to know a little grammar*

Set off the appositive phrase with commas.

*To punctuate correctly, you need to know a little grammar*

## 3. Look for prepositional phrases in THE BEGINNING OF THE SENTENCE.

If you find two CONSECUTIVE prepositional phrases AT THE BEGINNING of the sentence, then go past the prepositional phrases and see if the next word is the subject of the sentence. If so, put a comma after the prepositional phrases and before the subject.

Put your prepositional phrase memory sentence here as a test of this tip.

*In my room under my bed, you'll find my geometry textbook*

## 4. Look for an infinitive phrase (which starts with "to") at the beginning of the sentence and if it is not followed by a verb, put a comma after the phrase.

Got it? Next up is the Mastery Phrase Exercise.

# Lesson 9: Mastery Phrase Exercise

**Exercise 14:** Now let's review all our phrases. Look at the sentences below and do the following:

A. **Underline the phrase**
B. **Write the type of the phrase over the words**
C. **Put in commas if necessary and circle the commas. If no comma is necessary, put NC in front of the sentence.**

(You don't have to identify every prepositional phrase—just the ones that require you to apply the Prepositional Phrase Mastery Rule. If you are having trouble with this exercise, go to my Phrase Tips on the previous two pages.)

1. After the game we're going to Jo-Jo's.

2. Running past the office, I saw Miss Klekamp through the window.

3. In the morning after breakfast with Jerry I'll call you.

4. Miss Meyer my Religion teacher is substituting for Mr. Greimann.

5. Running for exercise is not one of my favorite activities.

6. I left your key under my car in the student parking lot.

# CHAPTER 3: PUNCTUATING PHRASES

7. Castling early in the game is a good chess maneuver. C

8. *The Adventures of Huckleberry Finn,* my favorite novel, is banned in lots of schools.

9. In the cupboard on the third shelf, you'll find some plastic forks.

10. Sweating like a banshee, I called her up and asked her to the dance.

11. Fred, spilling Coke on the new carpet, burst into the basketball meeting.

12. Inside my purse, at the end of the table, is your watch.

13. I called my English teacher, hoping he'd help me.

14. International Falls, the coldest town in the United States, is located 10 miles from Canada.

15. I gave the letter of recommendation to Mrs. Criswell, the Director of Admissions.

16. To prepare for the verbal section of the SAT, you need to know a lot of vocabulary.

## LESSON 9: MASTERY PHRASE EXERCISE

17. Strolling down the icy boulevard, she encountered a man with no shoes. C
___

18. To depend too much on other people, may be hazardous to your sense of independence. C
___

Hey Clamdiggers: I've been working you guys pretty hard. We have just learned a huge chunk of material. What do you say we take a little break? Maybe your teacher can play the James Brown track and put out some refreshments. I say it is time to relax. Maybe we can push the chairs back and Giovanni will show us how to do the party rock. What do you say, G-man?

### Exercise 15: Chapter 3 Review

Are You REALLY Still With Me?
___

1. What is the difference between simple and complex grammar pieces?
   *Complex is harder to find compared to simple.*

2. What is the definition of a phrase?
   *A part of a sentence that is seperat from the rest*

# CHAPTER 3: PUNCTUATING PHRASES

3. What are the two essential parts of a prepositional phrase?

Preposition and a noun or pronoun two

The optional parts?

between

4. List 10 prepositions from memory.

above, in, into, left, right, up, down, through, across, along

5. What two functions does a prepositional phrase do?

Adjectives and Adverbs

6. What are the five functions of an adverb prepositional phrase? (Which one is new?)

where, when, how, to what extent, and Why

7. What is the Prepositional Phrase Mastery Comma Rule?

Whenever you have two or more prepositional phrases at the beginning of the sentences, set them off with a comma.

## LESSON 9: MASTERY PHRASE EXERCISE

8. What is an exception to the Prepositional Phrase Mastery Comma Rule?
   *In some cases involving the word be the positions of the subject and verb are reversed*

9. Is there a comma in the following sentence and why and what is the subject in that sentence? (Careful!!)

   **After the game go right home.**
   *game because they are at a game*

10. What are the objective forms of the following:

    I    Me

    we   Us

    she  Her

    he   Him

    they Them

    you  You*

11. What is the "I/Me Rule"?
    *Subject/Object*

## CHAPTER 3: PUNCTUATING PHRASES

12. What are three places in the sentence where you can find a pronoun?
    beginning, end, and object of the prep

13. What amazing things can a writer do with a participial phrase?
    Change the tone of the sentence

14. What is the Participial Phrase Mastery Comma Rule?
    Set off any Participial Phrase with a comma.

15. Where can you find a participial phrase in a sentence? (3 places) Show me how to punctuate the phrase in each case.
    beginning, right after the beginning, and end

16. How do you avoid a dangling modifier?
    Put the subject right after the participial phrase

LESSON 9: MASTERY PHRASE EXERCISE

17. What is the Prepositional Phrase Memory Sentence?
In my room under my bed, you'll find my geometry textbook.

18. What is the Past Participial Phrase Memory Sentence?
Insulted by the tone of his voice, she hit the end button on the phone.

19. What is the Present Participial Phrase Memory Sentence?
Smiling like a cheshire cat, she slammed the door in my face.

20. Give me two past participles.
She has water a lot.

She has cake a lot.

21. Give me two present participles.
She has been quiet a lot.

She has been good a lot.

## CHAPTER 3: PUNCTUATING PHRASES

22. What is the function of a gerund phrase?
    Replace it with what

23. What is the Gerund Phrase Mastery Comma Rule?
    No comma

24. What is the Gerund Phrase Memory Sentence?
    Running across LBJ is not a smart idea

25. What is the tip for spotting a participial phrase?
    The word what makes no sense

26. What is the function of an appositive phrase?
    They restate the noun

## LESSON 9: MASTERY PHRASE EXERCISE

27. Where is an appositive phrase found?
    after a subject

28. What is the Appositive Phrase Memory Sentence?
    Mr. Lund, my clamdigging teacher, comes from Chicago

29. What is the Appositive Phrase Mastery Comma Rule?
    Set off all with a comma

30. What is the Infinitive Phrase Mastery Comma Rule?
    To punctuate correctly, you need to know a little grammar

31. What is the exception to the Infinitive Phrase Mastery Comma Rule?
    Do not put comma after phrase if followed by a verb.

## CHAPTER 4: PUNCTUATING CLAUSES

32. When you are trying to identify phrases, what should you look for first, second, third?
    The subject, verb, and preticit,

33. What is the hardest part for you in punctuating phrases?
    remembering then

CHAPTER 4

# Punctuating Clauses

# Lesson 1: Welcome to the World of C L A U S E S!

A **clause** is a group of words with a SUBJECT and a VERB.

"Does that mean a sentence is a clause, Mr. Lund?"

"Well, uhhhhh—yes, Kristy. A sentence IS a clause, but a clause is not always a sentence. Let me show you this."

Although I was late for the exam.

I was late for the exam.

One of the clauses above is not a sentence; please put a * in front of it.

"See what I mean when I say a sentence is always a clause but a clause is not always a sentence? For you Geometry fans, that is like saying that a *square is always a rectangle but a rectangle is not always a square.* Do you see that? That's logic."

CHAPTER 4: PUNCTUATING CLAUSES

## THREE KINDS OF CLAUSES

There are THREE kinds of clauses: **Adverb, Adjective and Noun clauses**. You use them all the time, I promise. All I need to do is help you recognize them when you use them so you know how to handle them correctly and punctuate them in your writing.

Here's a sentence that contains all three types:

**Adverb Clause**      **Noun Clause**
**Although I didn't know who she was, I knew that she was the one**
**Adjective Clause**
**who was in charge of my schedule.**

**Confused?** Don't worry. When you are done with this unit, you will be able to pick out each type and punctuate each of them correctly. I promise!

There are two mastery reasons for understanding English clauses:

1. To know how to punctuate them
2. To know how to correct sentence fragments

## LESSON 1: WELCOME TO THE WORLD OF C L A U S E S!

Probably the easiest clause is the Adverb Clause and that's where we begin. An adverb clause ALWAYS begins with one of the following words and since I know how unhappy Mr. Felix gets when I use hard grammar words (like—close your ears, buddy— 'subordinating conjunctions'), in honor of Felix I'm going to make up a **new name** for words that **begin adverb clauses**. Let's call them **Adverb Clause Words**.

---

### ADVERB CLAUSE WORD LIST
### (SUBORDINATING CONJUNCTIONS)

**WARNING:**
YOU **HAVE TO MEMORIZE** THESE WORDS!

After
Although, Though, *As though, Even though
As, *As if, If,
Unless, Because
Before
Since
Until, When, Whenever, While

*Do not use these adverb clauses **in the beginning of the sentence**.

---

Examples:
I felt as if I would choke.     Good
As if I would choke, I felt.    Not good!

Do you see what I mean? It doesn't work at the beginning of the sentence.

---

# CHAPTER 4: PUNCTUATING CLAUSES

## ADVERB CLAUSES

"Let's try to make a few clauses with these adverb clause words."

1. This is a clause:       After you leave the party
2. This is not a clause:   After the party

"Why isn't the second one a clause, Felix?"

"Don't know? Kristy, do you know why?"

"The second one is a prepositional phrase. It doesn't have a subject and a verb like the first one."

"Okay, that is a great point that Kristy is making. **BE CAREFUL!** Some of these adverb clause words can also be prepositions. Here they are: **AFTER, BEFORE, SINCE, UNTIL.**"

**Remember**: A *clause* must have both a *subject* and a *verb*.

```
                           S      V
```
1. This is a clause:       After you leave the party
2. This is not a clause:   After the party (prepositional phrase)

Exercise 1: Now look at the following groups of words and put a **CL** in front of the sentence if the group of words is a clause. (To be sure it is a clause, put an **S** over the subject and a **V** over the verb.)

### LESSON 1: WELCOME TO THE WORLD OF C L A U S E S!

1. until Sunday

CL 2. since he's written me
            S     V

3. before 6:00

CL 4. before you come
         S   V

5. until Friday

CL 6. after you finish the book
         S   V

7. after your English class

### WARNING:

Be sure you have memorized the list of adverb clause words (above) before you do the next exercise. TOMORROW WE WILL HAVE A MASTERY TEST ON THESE WORDS. Here's another copy of the words.

---

### ADVERB CLAUSE WORD LIST
### (SUBORDINATING CONJUNCTIONS)

After
Although, Though, *As though, Even though,
As, *As if, If,
Unless, Because
Before
Since
Until, When, Whenever, While

---

# CHAPTER 4: PUNCTUATING CLAUSES

**Exercise 2**: Underline the adverb clauses in the following sentences. Circle the adverb clause word and put **S** above the subject in the clause and **V** above the verb. Careful, there's at least one distracter in there.

1. I hate it (when) she looks at me like that.
2. (Whenever) I see her I get nervous.
3. I'm going to the party (even though) I'm sick.
4. She's not going to the dance (because) he asked someone else.
5. She talks (as if) she owned the place
6. She said that he was no longer welcome in his house.

"Do you see which one doesn't belong, Giovanni?"

"No, I didn't. They all look like they have adverb clauses to me."

"What's the adverb clause in #6, may I ask?"

"'That he was no longer welcome in his house.'"

"Are you sure? What's the **adverb clause word**?"

"'That.'"

"Is it on the adverb clause list? Check it out right now."

"No, I see it's not on there. Sorry."

## LESSON 1: WELCOME TO THE WORLD OF C L A U S E S!

"That's okay, Giovanni. It allows me to make a huge point now before we get too far into these difficult clauses."

### Professional Clamdigging Tip

It won't help you to learn the comma rules for clauses if you don't memorize the clause words that go with the rules.

"Also, did you notice that the **adverb clause** sometimes comes at the beginning of the sentence and sometimes at the end? Look at the sentences again in Exercise 2. What's a sentence with the adverb clause in the beginning, Kristy?"

"Number two. 'Whenever I see her, I get angry.'"

"Good, and where's a sentence with the adverb clause at the end?"

"Number three. 'I'm going to the party even though I'm sick.'"

### Professional Clamdigging Tip

Be sure to notice where the adverb clause is because that will determine whether you have a comma or not.

## CHAPTER 4: PUNCTUATING CLAUSES

"Anyone remember where this was true in phrases (Chapter 3)? Felix?"

> "Yeah, if the prepositional phrase is in the beginning of the sentence, we have a comma; if not, there's no comma."

"That's my Felix! You are really nailing this stuff down. I'm proud of you, buddy."

# Lesson 2: The Adverb Clause Comma Rule and Memory Sentence

## Professional Clamdigging™ Mastery Rule:

### Adverb Clause Comma Rule

Put a comma after an introductory adverb clause; DO NOT use a comma if the adverb clause comes at the end of the sentence.

## Professional Clamdigging™ Memory Sentence

### The Adverb Clause Memory Sentence

Whenever I see an adverb clause at the beginning of a sentence, I put a comma right after it.

## CHAPTER 4: PUNCTUATING CLAUSES

Exercise 3: Now let's put commas in the same sentences that we looked at in Exercise 2, and I have eliminated the sentence that does not have the adverb clause. Put commas after adverb clauses in the beginning of the sentence and please circle the comma so that everyone can see it. If the sentence does not need a comma, put **NC** in front of the sentence.

1. I hate it when she looks at me like that.

2. Whenever, I see her I get nervous.

3. I'm going to the party even though I'm sick.

4. She's not going to the dance because Charley asked someone else.

5. She talks as if she owned the place.

Check your answers with your teacher.

"Now, put your thinking caps on, Clamdiggers: let's dig deep into these adverb clauses for a minute. Why do you think we call these clauses **adverb clauses**? What does adverb mean? What does an adverb do? **What questions does an adverb answer**? Do you need to check the *Magical Wheel of Function* (p. 14)? Kristy?"

"Adverbs modify verbs, and adjectives and other adverbs."

"Okay and what questions do they answer, Giovanni?"

"Where, how, when, to what extent and why.'"

"Okay, very good. And now we need to add just one more question so that we can handle all the information that comes with adverb clauses. That is **'under what conditions?'**"

## LESSON 2: THE ADVERB CLAUSE COMMA RULE AND MEMORY SENTENCE

So here are the
**Six adverb clause questions:**

**1. Where?
2. When?
3. How?
4. To What Extent?
5. Why?
6. Under What Conditions?**

---

"I would like us to figure out the adverb questions that are in the five sentences above, but they are kind of tricky and so this time, instead of asking you to do them as an exercise, I want us to do them together. Is that okay, Felix?"

"Yeah, I was hoping you'd say that, Mr. Lund."

"Okay, Felix—you're up to bat first. What's the question in number one? Go ahead and read the sentence and then tell us the question."

"'I hate it when she looks at me like that.' Is it '**when**'—when she looks at me like that?"

"Kristy, do you agree?"

"I think it's '**why**'. Why do you hate it?"

"Could it be '**under what conditions**,' Mr. Lund?"

## CHAPTER 4: PUNCTUATING CLAUSES

"Actually, any of those questions works fine. So you see there a multiple possibilities now."

"What's the second one, Giovanni?"

"'**Under what conditions**.' I get nervous under what conditions?"

"Ok, good. Number three, Felix?"

"I think it could be either "**how**" or "**under what conditions**".  I'm going to the party how? Or I'm going to the party under what conditions?"

"Ok, can you do number four, Kristy?"

"Sure, it's '**why**'? She's not going to the dance—why? 'Because Charley, the JERK, asked someone else.'"

"Okay, let's get personal why don't we? Maybe Charley's a friend of mine. And the last one, Felix?"

"It's '**how**.' How does she talk?"

"Very good, everybody. **Tomorrow we have a mastery exam with adverb clauses words.** Don't forget!

## LESSON 2: THE ADVERB CLAUSE COMMA RULE AND MEMORY SENTENCE

**Exercise 4:** Write about a <u>funny thing</u> or a <u>sad thing</u> that happened to you or someone else. Use all 16 of the adverb clause words and underline them. Write the paragraph without looking at the list if at all possible. If the sentence you are writing requires a comma, put **C** at the beginning. If the sentence does not require a comma, put **NC** in front of it.

<u>After</u> school my friends and me stayed for soccer <u>when</u> one of us made a joke everyone burst out in laughter. <u>Even though</u> it wasn't that funny we laught <u>until</u> we couldn't anymore. <u>Whenever</u> someone else made a joke after that we couldn't though. <u>Although</u> they were even more funny. <u>Since</u> soccer was almost done we waited <u>while</u> our parents came. <u>Before</u> we left <u>though</u> it was late <u>as if</u> we cared. We stayed for a while more <u>as</u> it was fun. <u>Because</u> of us staying late we would and <u>if</u> we ever did this again it would be <u>As though</u> we were still friends. <u>Unless</u> we didn't.

See you Clamdiggers tomorrow!

# CHAPTER 4: PUNCTUATING CLAUSES

# Lesson 3: Busting Sentence Fragments

Ready for your first clause quiz?

**Exercise 5:** What is a clause? What is an adverb clause? Write out the adverb clause words (or subordinating conjunctions) in English (at least 16).

1. After
2. Although
3. Though
4. As Though
5. Even though
6. As
7. As if
8. if
9. Unless
10. Because
11. Before
12. Since
13. Until
14. When
15. Whenever
16. While

# LESSON 3: BUSTING SENTENCE FRAGMENTS

**Exercise 6:** Underline the adverb clauses in the following sentences. Then put in commas where they are necessary (and circle the commas—to show everyone that you mean business when it comes to commas). If no comma is necessary, put OK in front of the sentence. (By the way, there are two non-clause commas that are required. I just thought I'd warn you. Please put a big ☐ in front of those sentences and thank you kindly!)

1. <u>After you finish</u>, your essay show it to me.

2. <u>Although he likes</u>, her he doesn't have the nerve to talk to her.

OK 3. He acts <u>as if he's</u> president of the class.

4. <u>If you don't</u>, call me I'll call you.

5. After breakfast on Saturday, I'm leaving for a trip to New Orleans.

OK 6. We can leave <u>whenever you get</u> to my house.

☐ 7. Sprinting down the hall to beat the bell, I smashed head first into Mr. Greimann.

OK 8. I'm not going to the State Fair <u>unless you do</u>.

9. <u>Before you leave</u>, this afternoon stop by my locker.

☐ 10. <u>As I was turning the corner</u>, I lost control of my car.

---

Okay, Clamdiggers of the World Unite:

# CHAPTER 4: PUNCTUATING CLAUSES

Now we're ready to deal with another mastery rule (**Fixing Sentence Fragments**). This is something that drives English teachers and other literate readers of English up the wall. So our motto is:

## BE KIND TO YOUR READER—FIX YOUR FRAGMENTS.

(In case you're interested, the runner-up motto was: "Down with Sentence Terrorism." That got voted down—"way too violent," my Clamdiggers told me.)

Look at the following sentence:

**1. Before I left the house, I remembered to put the cat food in the refrigerator.**

"Underline the adverb clause in the sentence. Notice that this sentence really has two parts. One of the parts can stand alone as a complete sentence. (Does this sound like fifth grade English or what?) Which one is it? Felix! Take your time in answering the question, buddy; there is big money involved here! Felix, are you ready with an answer?"

**"I remembered to put the cat food in the refrigerator."**

"Okay, that gets you a piece of watermelon pie. Now everyone go up to sentence #1 and write the words **Independent Clause** above that clause."

**Independent Clause**
**"I remembered to put the cat food in the refrigerator."**

"The other part cannot stand alone. What is that part and what is wrong with it, Mr. Giovanni?"

**"Before I left the house…"**

"So what's wrong with that, Giovanni?"

## LESSON 3: BUSTING SENTENCE FRAGMENTS

"It's not complete. It needs something else. What did you do before you left the house?"

"You're starting to sound like an English teacher, G-man. You may have a career there. Okay, let's put that clause down too and write the words **Dependent Clause** over that one. Here we see that one of the clauses is a sentence (meaning it can stand alone) and the other one is a clause and not a sentence—so it cannot stand alone. Or to put it in another way, it is a sentence fragment."

**Dependent Clause (fragment)**
Before I left the house. . . .

Notice the dependent clause is ALSO the adverb clause. Don't be confused by this. Let me repeat: **DON'T BE CONFUSED BY THIS.** This is where 64.7% of my students give up on trying to understand clauses. Remember: there are only **three kinds of clauses: Adverb Clauses, Adjective Clauses, and Noun Clauses**. Right now, we are just looking at the adverb clause in a different way. If it helps, just think of it this way:

# Professional Clamdigging™ Mastery Rule:

### Adverb Clause Completeness Mastery Rule

An adverb clause must always be completed by another independent clause.

## CHAPTER 4: PUNCTUATING CLAUSES

Everyone look at this sentence:

***If I wanted to explain this to you.**

"Whoa! Time out! Finish that sentence, Mr. Lund, will you?"

"Calm down, Kristy. What's the big deal?"

"The **BIG DEAL** is that what you wrote there doesn't make any sense at all."

"Why not?"

"Because it is a fragment. It's incomplete!"

"So is that a dependent clause or an independent clause, Felix?"

"It's dependent."

**Dependent Clause (fragment)**
***If I wanted to explain this to you.**

"Can you finish it by adding an independent clause, Giovanni?"

        **Dependent Clause    Independent Clause**
**"If I wanted to explain this to you, I would do it."**

"Kristy, are you happy with that now? Do you need to take a walk around the block?"

"No, thanks. That's much better. My blood pressure is back to normal."

Do you see that the clause "if I wanted to explain this to you" is an **adverb clause**, and it is also a **dependent clause**?

## LESSON 3: BUSTING SENTENCE FRAGMENTS

There's nothing to be afraid of here. It's just taking something you know and putting it into a different context so you can connect it with some other useful information. You know what the sun is, of course. Now when your teacher told you in second grade that the sun was really considered a star, you didn't have trouble with that, did you? You could follow that train of thought—that the sun is the sun and it is also a star? See what I mean? You can handle the **adverb clause** as an **adverb clause** and also as a **dependent clause**. Good job. Congratulations!

**Exercise 7:** Now, look at the following clauses. Put an I in front of the independent clauses and put a D in front of the dependent clauses. [Hint: the dependent clause always begins with an adverb clause word (subordinating conjunction)]. Then decide if the sentence is good or a fragment. (Hint: if the sentence has a dependent clause and not an independent clause, it is called a fragment.) Put an OK in front of a good sentence and Frag in front of a fragment.

____D____  1. After he slugged me

____OK____ 2. I don't know anything about German history

____D____  3. As if she knows everything I'm going through

____D____  4. Whenever I see her

____OK____ 5. That new car is out of this world

____D____  6. After I turned him in

____D____  7. Even though it's time to go

Check your answers with the boss!

# CHAPTER 4: PUNCTUATING CLAUSES

By the way, putting a period after a dependent clause does not fool anyone into believing that it is a complete sentence. Usually we call this a sentence fragment or an incomplete sentence.

"How do you correct this kind of fragment, Giovanni?"

Even though it's time to go.*

> "Add an independent clause."

"Be my guest and do it, please!"

> "Even though it's time to go, I'm going to stay a bit more."

"Very good. Actually there is another kind of tricky way to fix the fragment—without adding an independent clause. Does anyone see that? Yes, Kristy?"

> "Remove the adverb clause word."

~~Even though~~ [I]t's time to go.

"Very clever, Kristy. If it's okay with your mother, you can take the rest of the week off!"

> **Exercise 8:** The paragraph below contains some errors in sentence structure (fragments) and in punctuation. Do the following to correct it:
>
> a. Underline each adverb clause
> b. Put in any commas that are required by the Adverb Clause Completeness Mastery Rule.
> c. Put an * in front of any sentence fragment.

## LESSON 3: BUSTING SENTENCE FRAGMENTS

   d. Rewrite the paragraph, putting in any necessary commas and add any necessary independent clauses.

Whenever I call her I get a dry throat and sweaty palms. Whenever I see her or hear her voice or see a picture of her. I can't speak. I feel like an idiot even though I'm a straight A student. After I called her last week I was so embarrassed that I promised I'd never talk to her again. Unless she called me. If I can't even carry on an intelligent conversation for fifteen minutes on a subject like math or biology which are my best subjects. As if I didn't get enough sleep. After she asked me for help in Economics I couldn't even say yes. I just nodded. Although I was dying to tell her anything she wanted to know.
(You can write on this page and the next page too.)

# CHAPTER 4: PUNCTUATING CLAUSES

Finis. That's all, folks. See you tomorrow.

# Lesson 4: 'Kicking the Tires' of Adjective Clauses

Okay, Clamdiggers of the World—the second clause we will study is the Adjective Clause. Do you want the good news or the bad news on Adjective Clauses?

"I want the bad news."

"Kristy, I would have taken you for the good news crowd. The bad news is that the sky is falling. The good news is . . . Do you want to hear the good news?"

"Sure."

"It's going to take a couple hundred thousand years."

"Very funny! What's the bad news about **Adjective Clauses**?"

"The bad news is that some Adjective Clauses take commas and some do NOT take commas, so you need to really pay attention to this one."

"And the good news, Mr. Lund?"

"The good news is that there are not nearly as many Adjective Clause Words to memorize."

First let's look at four adjective clauses:

1. He's the guy **WHO** plays bass in our group.

2. He's the guy **THAT** plays bass in our group.

3. The convertible is the car **WHICH** I'd love to rent.

# CHAPTER 4: PUNCTUATING CLAUSES

**4. The convertible is the car THAT I'd love to rent.**

"What are the Adjective Words in those sentences, Felix?"

"'Who,' 'that,' and 'which.'"

"Okay, can you all please take a deep breath? I need to tell you something that is potentially upsetting."

**Another word for Adjective Clause Words is Relative Pronouns.** That's the term that most grammar books like to use.

**Adjective Clause Words = Relative Pronouns**

Notice we use **who** and **that** for a person (guy) and **which** and **that** for a thing (Lamborghini).

"Which guy is he—the guy who plays bass."

"And #3, G-man?"

"Which car do you want to rent."

"Do those sound like adjective questions, Mr. Felix?"

## LESSON 4: 'KICKING THE TIRES' OF ADJECTIVE CLAUSES

"Yes. And they modify nouns or pronouns. Let's get show on the road, Mr. Lund."

"Whoa! Now you're answering questions that I didn't even ask. You've been hanging around Kristy too much, I think! All right—just one more question and then we'll put Felix's impatience out of commission. What is the definition of a clause, Felix?"

"Uh, a group of words with a subject and a verb."

"That's good for 10 bonus points on your next exam."

Okay, a clause has to have a subject and a verb. Put '**S**' and '**V**' over the subjects and verbs in each clause.

### Professional Clamdigging Tip

Don't forget that the Adjective Clause words—**who, which**, and **that** are also called **relative pronouns**. Did you hear that? PRONOUNS!!!

Let's let Felix go first. Look at the adjective clause sentence #1. What is the subject and what is the verb in that clause?

1. He's the guy **WHO** plays bass in our group.

"The verb is 'plays.' I'm not sure what the subject is. But I can see that Kristy knows. Why don't you ask her?"

# CHAPTER 4: PUNCTUATING CLAUSES

"He just told you that the Adjective Clause Words were Relative Pronouns, that is the subject of the clause."

"Okay, Kristy. Patience is a virtue too—in addition to grammar expertise. Do you see the subject now, Felix?"

"Is it 'who'?"

"Correctomundo! Now tell us the **subjects** and **verbs** in each Adjective Clause."

**S**=Subject  **V**=Verb

 **S**  **V**
who plays bass in the group

 **S**  **V**
that plays bass in the group

    **S V**
which I'd love to rent

   **S V**
that I'd love to rent

By the way, **adjective clauses** are also known as **relative clauses**. There you are—more name switching from these magical English teachers. BUT, in this *Guide to Professional Clamdigging*™, we will call them **ADJECTIVE CLAUSES**—period!

But remember, to preserve your sanity—there in the *REAL* world:

**adjective clauses = relative clauses**

This is where another 26.2% of my students give up on learning clauses.

# LESSON 4: 'KICKING THE TIRES' OF ADJECTIVE CLAUSES

**Exercise 9**: Underline the adjective clause in the following sentences and circle the adjective clause word and then put '**S**' above the subject in the adjective clause and '**V**' above the verb in the clause.

1. That's the building that is my all-time favorite in the city of Dallas.
2. I gave the homework to Mrs. Gustafson, the lady who is tutoring Jim.
3. He's the guy who plays point guard on our basketball team.
4. This is the best essay that I have read this year.
5. I called Sharon, who is my oldest sister.
6. I can't find the guy that sold me the suit.
7. Mr. Couser, who is the Career Counselor at the school, also teaches Psychology.
8. Giovanni, who lives in Dallas, is originally from Italy.
9. Just ask Felix, who is wearing the red and white checked shirt.
10. Kristy is the girl that I'm recommending to you as a tutor.

**Check your answers with your favorite teacher!**

CHAPTER 4: PUNCTUATING CLAUSES

# Lesson 5: 'Who' versus the HATED 'Whom'!

"There is another **Adjective Clause word** (relative pronoun) that I'll teach you in a few minutes. But this can be a little painful, so I want a nice long runway for this plane to come down on—if you know what I mean. Don't worry, Felix—no crash landings this time around!"

Okay, let's do it this way. Look at the clauses below and circle the adjective clause in the following sentences and draw an arrow to the word it modifies. Then find the subject 'S' and the verb 'V' in each clause:

1. That's the audio speaker WHICH IS BROKEN.

2. That's the audio speaker WHICH I FIXED.

"What word is the clause referring to in the first sentence, Giovanni?"

"'Speaker.'"

"Good, and the second sentence?"

"'Speaker' also."

"And what are the subjects in the two sentences, may I ask, G-man?"

"'Which.'"

"Uh, I'm afraid not for number 2. Fasten your seat belts, everyone. This is where we start to encounter some bad weather on our journey. Anyone else? Kristy?"

## LESSON 5: 'WHO' VERSUS THE HATED 'WHOM'!

"'Which' is the subject of #1. 'I' is the subject of #2."

"Now how the heck do you know that, Kristy?"

"Because we know that 'I' is the subject—that's easy to see."

"And the verbs? What are they in #1 and #2?"

"'Is' and 'fixed.'"

"That's right."

**Here is the correct information about those clauses:**

                          S   V

1. That's the audio speaker WHICH IS BROKEN.

                                S  V

2. That's the audio speaker WHICH I FIXED.

"Can anyone see why 'which' is the subject in one clause and not the other? Felix?"

"I think so. In the first sentence the clause is about the speaker. In the second sentence the clause is about the person that fixed the speaker."

"You know what, Felix? That is great thinking. You get 'Plus 10' on the next exam. Giovanni?"

"Okay, I get it now! So 'which' is the subject of the clause in #1 and the object of the clause in #2."

## CHAPTER 4: PUNCTUATING CLAUSES

"Holy smokes! That's right. Plus 10 for you too, Giovanni! I thought I was going to have to give you a long, boring explanation of this and look at that—you guys figured it out on your own."

                                                       S  V

1. That's the audio speaker WHICH IS BROKEN.

                S    V

    (The speaker is broken)

                                          O  S  V

2. That's the audio speaker WHICH I FIXED.

        S  V      O

    (I fixed the speaker)

"So you see that the Adjective Clause word (relative pronoun) can be the subject or the object of the clause. Now, remember: **THAT IS NOT THE SAME AS SUBJECT OR OBJECT OF THE WHOLE SENTENCE.** What are the subjects and verbs of the sentences in #1 and #2? Kristy, do you want to get it on the action?"

"'That' is the subject in both cases and 'is' is the verb in both cases."

"All right, have it your way—Plus 10 for you too, Kristy."

**REMEMBER:**
A CLAUSE IS NOT ALWAYS A SENTENCE,
BUT A SENTENCE IS ALWAYS A CLAUSE.

---

**Exercise 10:** Put **S** or **O** over the Adjective Clause Words (relative pronouns) in the following adjective clauses to show whether the Adjective Clause Word is a subject on an object in that clause. **When you're done with those, go back to Exercise 9 and find the TWO items where the Adjective Clause**

## LESSON 5: 'WHO' VERSUS THE HATED 'WHOM'!

**Word is an object and write those in the blanks below for #5 and #6.**

1. that I gave her
   The joke that I gave her is gone.

2. which amazed me.
   The sandwhich which amazed me was so good.

3. who calls me every Sunday afternoon
   Mom who calls me every Sunday afternoon

4. that I love to talk to.
   My friends that I love to talk to

5. 

6. 

Check your answers with the chief (or jefe, if you prefer Spanish)!

---

**Exercise 10B:** Now make up complete sentences that include these adjective clauses in #1-4.

1. The necklace that I gave her she like which amazed me.

2. My mom who calls me every Sunday afternoon that I love to talk to.

## CHAPTER 4: PUNCTUATING CLAUSES

3. _____
   _____

4. _____
   _____

**Check your answers with your teacher please!**

---

"Okay, Clamdiggers—I want to check one thing in Exercise 10, but before I do that, I've got to tell you that we are going to **ce-le-brate** at the end of Adjective Clauses! I was going to wait until the end of the chapter, but you guys really have gotten 'on the Clamdigging bus,' and I am absolutely thrilled to be in the same room with you and see how you are getting this stuff! Yes, Felix?"

   "Are we going to listen to more 'Soul' music from the 60s, Mr. Lund?"

"Well, I think I'm going to hold on to my world famous poker face and keep you guys in suspense about that. But I will tell you that we are moving to the 70s for this music. And you are going to love it, Felix!"

"Let's go back to Exercise 10 for a second. What two sentences did you find in Exercise 9 where the Adjective Clause Word was an object? Giovanni? Did you find them?"

   "I think so—#4 and #10."

"Correctamundo, buddy!" Look at these:

**O  S  V**

a. This is the best essay that I have read this year. (I have read it.)

## LESSON 5: 'WHO' VERSUS THE HATED 'WHOM'!

              **O**   **S**     **V**

b. Kristy is the girl that I'm recommending to you as a tutor. (I am recommending her.)

Okay, everybody—here is the moment of truth. Pay attention! Notice that we use the word 'that' for an **OBJECT Adjective Clause Word** and we can also use the same word for the **SUBJECT Adjective Clause Word** as you will see in the following example.

              **S V**

c. This is the essay that is really good!

So, the word 'that' can be used as either a subject or an object in an adjective clause.

> "I'm sorry to complain, Mr. Lund, but this is starting to get a little tedious. If you can use the same word for each of them, then why does any of this really matter to us?"

"You know what, Felix—I'm not going to fuss at you this time. That is a valid point. What I just said about 'that' is true also of 'which'—you can use the same word for either the SUBJECT form or the OBJECT form."

**BUT IT IS NOT TRUE FOR 'WHO.'**

**WHO/WHOM** (Cue the Halloween music!)

---

*Professional Clamdigging* **Tip**

Use "who" for the subject adjective clause word and "whom" for the object adjective clause word.

# CHAPTER 4: PUNCTUATING CLAUSES

"So let's change the adverb clause word in B. from 'that' to 'who/whom.' Which one do we use, Felix?"

"Oh, I've never been able to understand this one."

"All right then, let's do it together. Here's the sentence."

         **O  S**     **V**
b. Kristy is the girl that I'm recommending to you as a tutor.
**(I am recommending her.)**

The *Professional Clamdigging™ Tip* says to use '**WHO**' for the subject Adjective Clause Word and '**WHOM**' for the object Adjective Clause Word. So which do we use here?

"Oh, I get it. It would be whom because we need the OBJECT word."

"Okay, put it in the sentence."

         **O  S**     **V**
Kristy is the girl (whom I'm recommending to you as a tutor).

"That's correct. And here's a sentence with the SUBJECT form."

         **S V**
Kristy is the girl (who likes to tutor).

"Felix, do I need to cancel the party? Are you lost? I want you *on* the Clamdigging Bus—not under it!"

"Uh, I think it's finally clear. Can we do a couple more examples, Mr. Lund?"

"You've got it, my man. Check out these two sentences. You tell me, Felix—which one is 'WHO' and which one is 'WHOM'?"

## LESSON 5: 'WHO' VERSUS THE HATED 'WHOM'!

1. He's the officer that gave me the ticket.

2. He's the officer that I hit at Forest and Abrams.

> "Okay, give me a second. Let's see—don't anyone say anything! In number one the officer gave me the ticket, so that's the subject form and so we use 'who.' In the second one, 'I hit the officer,' so that is object form and we use 'whom.'"

> 1. He's the officer **who** gave me the ticket.

> 2. He's the officer **whom** I hit at Forest and Abrams.

"You did it, Felix-meister! Hip-hip HOORAY!"

> "You mean that's IT, Mr. Lund? That's all that '**who/whom**' jazz is all about? I have never understood that."

"That's right. That's all that '**who/whom**' jazz is all about. No more, no less. Of course, notice you need to understand quite a bit of grammar to get it, right?"

> "Yeah, I could never get that subject/object stuff!"

"Well, Felix, you have another 20 point bonus on your next test, so that should keep your mother happy. Yes, Kristy—what's on your mind?"

> "I think I just figured out a trick for seeing which word to use (**WHO/WHOM**). If you look at the two sentences above, it's easy to see that the clause in the second sentence has a subject—'I,' so the Adjective Clause Word needs to be in the OBJECT form (**WHOM**). In number two, since we do not see a normal subject in the clause, the Adjective Clause Word (**WHO**) becomes the subject."

# CHAPTER 4: PUNCTUATING CLAUSES

"That is as smooth as ice cream dripping down a slippery sugar cone on a summer afternoon in Sweet Gum, Texas, Kristy. I think that I'm going to have to let you take the day off tomorrow."

"Wow, I like that sentence, Mr. Lund. Where did you learn to write like that?"

"Just use good 'pics' and 'jazz' and voice."

"Can you teach us to write with 'pics' and 'jazz' and voice, Mr. Lund?"

"Sure, that's in the next book*, Mr. Felix. I'd love to have you on that bus too."

*Writing Jazz: Mr. Lund's Guide to Professional Clamdigging™

**Let's try to apply Kristy's tip.**

**Exercise 11**: Reread Kristy's tip above and apply it to these four sentences to decide whether to choose WHO or WHOM.

1. I talked to the lady (who/**whom**) you recommended.

2. Give this paper to the person (**who**/whom) calls your name.

3. The bank officer (who/**whom**) you met just arrived from North Carolina.

4. The guy (**who**/whom) is standing over there by the window looks like a CIA agent.

# LESSON 5: 'WHO' VERSUS THE HATED 'WHOM'!

**Check in with your teacher about the answers before you catch the bus to the Botanical Garden!**

"Well, is Kristy's tip working for you, Giovanni?"

"Yeah, it is. I never thought that I'd get this WHO/WHOM lesson. Thanks, Kristy!"

"You're welcome, Giovanni!"

Okay, I want to do one last exercise for today and this time, I'm going to mix up the **adverb clauses** and the **adjective clauses**. This should bring everybody back to reality and keep you on your toes.

**Exercise 12:** Underline the clauses in the following sentences; then in front of the sentence put '**ADV**' if it contains an **adverb clause** and '**ADJ**' if it contains an **adjective clause**. Good luck, Clamdiggers!

ADV  1. <u>Whenever she asks</u> me a question, <u>I freeze up.</u>   (ADJ)

ADJ  2. The book <u>that I told you about</u> is checked out.

ADJ  3. I'll take you to the lady <u>who helped me.</u>

ADJ  4. Recommend someone <u>whom I can go to</u> for help.

ADV  5. She looks <u>as if she just woke up.</u>

ADV  6. I'm not going <u>if you don't.</u>

ADJ  7. That is the food <u>that I love.</u>

## CHAPTER 4: PUNCTUATING CLAUSES

**ADJ**   8. Give the money to the man <u>who is standing</u> by the door.

### Professional Clamdigging Tip

Notice the "**whom**" in #4 can be removed and the sentence will still make good sense:

**Recommend someone I can go to for help.**

This is called a **deep structure adjective clause**. In other words, even though **whom** or **that** do not appear on the surface, we feel that they are still there in the underlying structure of the sentence. It is almost like the understood **you**. When we say recommend, we are really saying YOU recommend…right? That's more *English magic* for you and don't get mad at me—I didn't invent the English language.

By the way, in addition to **who/whom/that/which**, there are a couple of other Adjective Clause words that are not quite as common. Underline the clauses in the following sentences, circle the relative pronouns, and then list them below.

1. That's the park **where** I used to play.

2. That's the person **whose** car I borrowed.

3. That was the day **when** everything went wrong.

Careful with #3! 'When' can also be an Adverb Clause Word.

## LESSON 5: 'WHO' VERSUS THE HATED 'WHOM'!

Notice the difference:

**adj clause**
That was the day when everything went wrong. (modifies noun 'day')

**adv clause**
When everything went wrong, we decided to leave. (modifies verb 'decided')

"Kristy? Got a question?"

"Yeah, I know how to use **who** and **whom**, but I've noticed that almost no one uses it correctly. Is it really necessary to use the word 'whom'?"

"Tell you the truth, Kristy, that is a hard question to answer honestly. This is one place where I would guess that the language is changing and I would be willing to bet that in another 50 years the word 'whom' may be like a dinosaur that nobody uses. As I've said before, I'm not telling you how to talk out there on the street—I'm telling you the rules of Standard English Grammar and Usage. But you are making a good point. And let me make a good point in return. There are errors and then there are **egregious** errors."

To **whom** are you speaking. (Correct but pretty rare.)

To **who** are you speaking. (Wrong and sounds terrible!)

**Who** are you speaking to? (NOT CORRECT, BUT the way most people would probably say it And notice, that was 'say it'. The standard for writing is still—**follow the rule**!)

So even though most of us shy away from 'whom,' we know when it should be used. That's the moral of the story at this stage in our linguistic history.

That's it for today. Go home and take it easy! Tomorrow's lesson is tough!

CHAPTER 4: PUNCTUATING CLAUSES

# Lesson 6: Restrictive and Non-Restrictive Adjective Clauses—Here Come the Commas!

Now we are ready to **punctuate adjective clauses**. I think that is the hardest Mastery Rule in the book, so fasten your seat belt!

Look at the following sentence and underline the adjective clause.

1. My truck, <u>which is a Nissan</u>, has 60,000 miles on it.

Now write the sentence below without the clause.
*My truck has 60,000 miles on it*

"What do you think, Felix—is your sentence drastically different from the original one above?"

"Not really. We just don't know what kind of truck it is."

"That's right—it could be a Ford or a Dodge or a Chevrolet, but that is clearly not the main thing in the sentence. Now look at sentence #2 and underline the adjective clause."

2. Never buy cars <u>that have over 200,000 miles on them</u>.
Now write the sentence out without the clause.
*Never buy cars*

"Is it much different from the one above, Kristy?"

"Yes, it is. It is kind of crazy to say 'Never buy cars.' But it is not crazy to say, 'Never buy cars that have over 200,000 miles on them.'"

That's right; the clause in #2 **is necessary to make sense.** This is because the clause

## LESSON 6: RESTRICTIVE AND NON-RESTRICTIVE ADJECTIVE CLAUSES

**restricts** the meaning of the cars (**to limit the meaning only to the undesirable or doubtful ones that you don't want to buy**). This **Adjective Clause is RESTRICTIVE or ESSENTIAL!**

Imagine a pie chart—cut into two parts. One side says: "Cars that have under 200,000 miles on them" and the other says "Cars that have more than 200,000 miles on them."

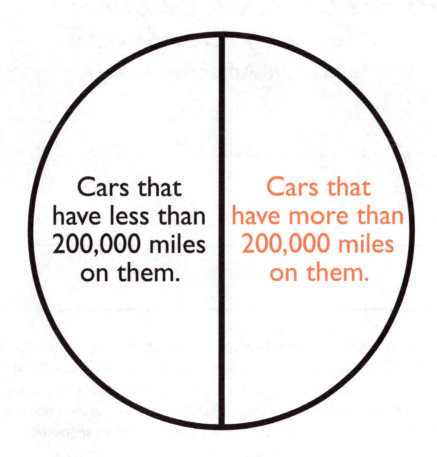

"Does it make a difference which one you choose, Giovanni? Would it matter to you?"

"Yeah, of course!"

Okay, that is because the **clause is restrictive**. It is restricting (or narrowing) the meaning

# CHAPTER 4: PUNCTUATING CLAUSES

to **under** or **over** 200,000 miles. And that is important or essential.

**AND** that is your memory sentence for a restrictive adjective clause:

*Professional Clamdigging™*
*Memory Sentence*
Restrictive Adjective Clause

Never buy a car **that has over 200,000 miles on it.**

---

## NON-RESTRICTIVE ADJECTIVE CLAUSE

---

The clause in #1 above, on the other hand, gives us ADDITIONAL information. The truck is a Nissan. But a Chevrolet or a Toyota or any truck COULD have 60,000 miles on it. So the clause does not really restrict or limit the meaning of truck. The fact is, you probably don't even need to know what kind of truck it is. All you need to know is that it is my truck. It just gives additional information about the noun, sort of like an appositive.

LESSON 6: RESTRICTIVE AND NON-RESTRICTIVE ADJECTIVE CLAUSES

## *Professional Clamdigging*™ *Memory Sentence*
### Non-Restrictive Adjective Clause

> My truck, **which is a Nissan**, has over 60,000 miles on it.

Because the information is extra or non-essential or non-restrictive, we need to set it off with commas.

"Giovanni, remind us: what is the **Appositive Memory Sentence?**"

"Mr. Lund, my Clamdigging teacher, comes from Chicago."

Notice that the appositive follows the same kind of logic. Since the information added is extra and non-essential or non-restrictive, there are commas. Let me try to say this in a cool and cute way to help you remember it.

### *Professional Clamdigging* Tip

> When the information in the clause is extra, then we add extra commas. When the information is not extra but essential and restrictive, then we do not use commas. So commas suggest less important information.

CHAPTER 4: PUNCTUATING CLAUSES

# Professional Clamdigging™ Mastery Rule:

## Adjective Clause Comma Rule

Use commas to set off a NON-RESTRICTIVE adjective clause. **Do not use commas with RESTRICTIVE adjective clauses.** Remember that the clause that takes commas has extra information like an appositive that can be left out without changing the meaning.

My friend, a student from Australia, lives in Plano. (appositive)

My friend, who is from Australia, lives in Plano. (non-restrictive adjective clause)

(By the way, before you start the next exercise, let me give you two other Professional Clamdigging™ tips to help you; at least they help **me** a lot.)

The word **that** in almost EVERY case introduces RESTRICTIVE clauses. So NO COMMAS!

## LESSON 6: RESTRICTIVE AND NON-RESTRICTIVE ADJECTIVE CLAUSES

**The assignment that you gave us yesterday was actually pretty easy.** (No commas!)

Whenever you see a common noun preceded by **'the,'** it is followed by a restrictive clause (NO COMMAS).

The money **which you gave me yesterday** is counterfeit. (restrictive clause)

The guy **that smiled at her** is the President of our senior class. (restrictive clause)

**Exercise 13**: Underline the Adjective Clauses in the following sentences and then put R for Restrictive and NR for Non-Restrictive above the clause. Then decide if you need commas or not. If so, put in the commas and circle them. If not, put NC in front of the number.

1. That pizza <u>that I got at Gino's</u> is not very fresh.
   R   NC

2. My new car, <u>which is a Toyota</u>, has a great navigator system.
   NR

3. Smart phones, <u>which cost hundreds of dollars</u>, now can do most computer functions.
   NR

## CHAPTER 4: PUNCTUATING CLAUSES

4. Janet, who is my best friend, lives in Mesquite.
   NR

5. Ms. Klekamp, who is from Illinois, is our principal.
   NR

6. My next door neighbor loaned me a book that I really want to read.
   R Nc

7. Students that do not do their homework are usually not very successful.
   R Nc

8. Mr. Fry, who is our basketball coach, loves the music of Tchaikovsky.
   NR

9. Tonight I'm making my wife's favorite Italian dish, which we picked up from a restaurant chef in Rome.
   NR

---

**Check out the answers with your teacher or at lovinggrammar.com.**

"See you guys tomorrow; I've got to get to the store: I'm cooking up something special tonight—my favorite meal."

"What is it, Mr. Lund?"

"Think about it, Felix, my man! All right, if you're not going to take a guess at it, I'll tell you: it's Linguine alle Vongole."

"What did you say?"

"Ask Giovanni after the class; he can translate that--or Google it or check it out on the Clamdigger website: lovinggrammar.com."

# Lesson 7: Lars and the Real Sentence— Commas That Can Change Reality!!!

Okay, today we are going to get into something really strange. We're going to see where commas can actually change reality. Before we get there, please look at this sentence.

**Ryan Gosling, who is the star of my favorite movie, is from Canada.**

*Professional Clamdigging* **Tip**

> When we put an adjective clause after a person's proper name, it is always extra or non-restrictive information. So we use commas!

"It's called *Lars and the Real Girl*, Kristy."

"What's it about?"

"It's about how a town that helps a guy who has some very serious issues of grief. I guess you could say it's kind of a fantasy world, like Shakespeare's *The Tempest*, but I think it is very powerful and moving. And, of course, it's very shocking—especially in the beginning!"

"What do you mean shocking?"

## CHAPTER 4: PUNCTUATING CLAUSES

"Well…how do I say this? If you check out the movie for about 20 minutes, you'll see what I mean. Just give it a chance to work through those weirdnessess, and then gradually you'll see something quite amazing happen to the people in the town—something very good, by the way. You will be wondering if that could ever happen to a real town, and if you're like me, you're wishing that it could. Let's get back to work."

Read these two sentences carefully. What's the difference between them?

A. My sister who lives in Minnesota is in advertising.

B. My sister, who lives in Minnesota, is in advertising.

"Giovanni?"

"No idea."

"Okay, Felix? Kristy? Nobody?"

"I'll give you a hint. The punctuation actually tells us how many sisters the speaker has. Can you figure it out? Come on, Kristy? Are you going to let your stellar reputation go to the dogs?"

"I get it now. In B. the speaker has only one sister, so it is extra information (**non-restrictive**) and we need commas. In A. the speaker has more than one sister and I guess only one of them lives in Minnesota, so the clause is **restrictive**."

"Right-oh! Giovanni?"

"I see what you mean. So in A. it says, 'my sister who lives in Minnesota is in advertising.' Then you could say, 'my sister who lives in Wisconsin is a lawyer and my sister who lives in Kansas is a nurse.'"

**LESSON 7: LARS AND THE REAL SENTENCE**

"That's it. You're on the Clamdigging Bus, baby. So therefore the adjective clause is **Restrictive/Essential/Necessary and Non-extra**, so there are no commas. But the commas in B. tell us that the speaker has only one sister. The fact that she lives in Minnesota is really just **extra** information. It doesn't matter really. (So we add **extra** commas.)"

---

**Exercise 14**: Write the difference in the following pairs of sentences.

1a. My car that is at the service station is leaking oil.

1b. My car, which is at the service station, is leaking oil.

Difference:
_____, which ,_____

2a. My son who is in kindergarten goes to Kirkwood Elementary School in Irving.

2b. My son, who is in kindergarten, goes to Kirkwood Elementary School in Irving.

Difference:
_____ , , _____

3a. The Dallas Lutheran School lawyer, who is in his 40s, plays tennis very well.

3b. The Dallas Lutheran School lawyer who is in his 40s plays tennis very well.

## CHAPTER 4: PUNCTUATING CLAUSES

Difference:

_____ , ,  _____
_____

**Check answers with your instructor. One more exercise to go and then we put the wrap on Adjective Clauses.**

---

Here's one other little problem that I want to introduce you to. Remember, we said that if a noun is preceded by 'the,' then the Adjective Clause following it is restrictive. Here were the examples:

**The** money **which you gave me yesterday** is counterfeit. (restrictive clause)

**The** guy **that smiled at her** is the President of our senior class. (restrictive clause)

"How about if we have a proper noun like a 7-Eleven store?"

"Is the clause in the following sentence restrictive or non-restrictive? Why?"

The 7-Eleven which is on Greenville Avenue is open 24 hours a day.

"Kristy?"

"I think that it would be non-restrictive (with commas) if there were only one store by that name. If there are multiple stores, then it is a restrictive clause (no commas)."

"That's right. You can see that in this sentence about another store of the same name."

# LESSON 6: RESTRICTIVE AND NON-RESTRICTIVE ADJECTIVE CLAUSES

The 7-Eleven which is on Arapaho Road is closed for repairs

"The Adjective clause is restrictive because otherwise how would we know which store is closed for repairs? So if it is restrictive, do we have commas or not, Felix?"

**"No commas, Mr. Lund!"**

One last exercise before we start to celebrate.

---

**Exercise 15**: Look at the following sentences and **underline** the clause in the sentence and then put in commas that are necessary. Put **NC** if no comma is necessary. **Warning:** there are both Adverb Clauses and Adjective Clauses in this exercise, so as they say in London: "Mind the Gap."

1. The last time, that I saw you, you were about four feet tall.

2. Whenever I forget, to turn off the AC the building supervisor checks my room.

3. My late wife, who was from Chicago, was a fantastic flamenco dancer.

4. You look, as if you could eat a horse.

5. Call me right, after you get home.

6. When I was, ten years old I met Jesse Owens who won three gold medals in 1936 in Nazi Germany.

7. The lady, who is over there by Paul, is a friend of my mother's.

8. If you can't, get this job done I'll find someone who can.

## CHAPTER 4: PUNCTUATING CLAUSES

9. I'll do it, when you give me the materials that I need for the job. **(Careful, there is a clause-within-a-clause in this sentence.)**

10. Is that the car that you were telling me about?
    NC

11. It was, as though we were all in a space capsule.

12. After you clean, the other desk you can go.

13. Tell me something that I don't know.
    NC

14. Sharon, who works in advertising, is always traveling somewhere.

15. The book, which you gave me, was fantastic.

16. You will not go to the party, until you clean your room.

17. The composer that I like most is Bach.
    NC

18. I have an autograph from Roberto Clemente, who played right field, for the Pirates.

19. Even though I did everything, that I could to be friends, she never noticed me. **(This also has a baby clause within a mama clause!)**

20. My new bicycle, which is from France is as light as a feather.

**Check your answers with the teacher!**

---

"Before we say goodbye to Adjective Clauses, I would like to suggest that we put on a little party music to celebrate — if your teacher has no objection, of course. This is not 'Soul' music—it is 'Disco' music from the late 70s. The tune is called 'Staying Alive'—by the Bee Gees. (You should have no problem finding it on YouTube.) See if your teacher can play it

## LESSON 7: LARS AND THE REAL SENTENCE

for you—preferably loudly. It's one of my favorite dance tunes, and, believe me, this music will keep you in motion! I'm sure you all know it. Yeah, I see that smile on Giovanni's face."

"And, by the way, you guys, I'm really proud of your hard work! One more clause to go— **Noun Clauses**—coming up! Have fun!"

CHAPTER 4: PUNCTUATING CLAUSES

# Lesson 8: Noun Clauses—"At Your Service!"

I've some great news for "youse" today. **The Noun Clauses** will be your favorites because all you have to remember is NO COMMAS with noun clauses. Does this remind you of any one of the phrase types?

Since I'm seeing a lot of blank faces instead of raised hands at the moment, I think my only recourse is to have a **POP QUIZ on MEMORY SENTENCES**. Here we go!

1. Prepositional Phrase

    *In my room under my bed, you'll find my geometry textbook.*

2. Past Participial Phrase

    *Insulted by the tone of his voice, she hit the end button on her cell phone.*

3. Present Participial Phrase

    *Smiling like a cheshire cat, she slammed the door in my face.*

4. Gerund Phrase

    *Running across LBJ is not a smart idea.*

5. Appositive Phrase

    *Mr. Lund, my chairdragging teacher, comes from Chicago.*

6. Infinitive Phrase

    *To punctuate correctly, you need to know a little grammar.*

## LESSON 8: NOUN CLAUSES—"AT YOUR SERVICE!"

"Now that you are tuned into the phrases, which one has no commas, Giovanni?"

"Gerunds."

"And what is the memory sentence for gerunds?"

"Running across LBJ is not a smart idea."

"Very good. And what grammar 'move' does the gerund phrase do, Kristy?"

"Noun."

"So what is that gerund doing in the memory sentence about the busy double-decker tollway in Dallas?"

"It's the subject."

"So gerund phrases and noun clauses do noun work—**noun moves**!"

Now, let's get philosophical for a moment: where are all the places that we can see **nouns** in English sentences? Look at these sentences:

1. John is late again.

2. John is a terrific student.

3. John gave Jenni a watch.

4. Jenni gave John a CD for his birthday.

"Let's go to work, Felix! Where are the nouns?"

### CHAPTER 4: PUNCTUATING CLAUSES

"John is the subject in #1 and #2 and #3. Student is the predicate noun in #2. Jenni is the Indirect Object in #3 and 'watch' is the Direct Object. And in #4 Jenni is the Subject and John is the Indirect Object."

"You forgot one. Mr. Giovanni, let's put the phone away. Kristy, what's the other one please?"

"'Birthday' is the Object of the Preposition."

Let's put down the positions in a sentence where we can we find a noun?

1. Subject (John in #1)
2. Predicate Noun (student in #2)
3. Direct Object (watch in #3)
4. Indirect Object (Jenni in #3)
5. Prepositional Phrase (birthday in #4)

# Professional Clamdigging™ Mastery Rule:

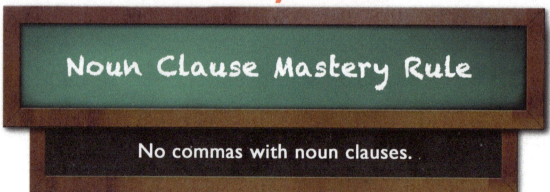

LESSON 8: NOUN CLAUSES—"AT YOUR SERVICE!"

"Now isn't that music to your ears, Felix?"

"Can we listen to more music, Mr. Lund?"

"Not now, buddy. So if we can find a noun in any of these five positions, then we can find a **NOUN CLAUSE** in any of these five positions, right?"

Next problem: **how do we spot a noun clause?**

Noun clauses usually begin with **question** words.

Let's look at an example.

What you see is a painting by Monet.

"What's the verb in this sentence, Felix?"

"'Is.'"

"Put a box around everything that comes before the verb. That, my friend, is the **noun clause** in this sentence. Tell us, Felix."

"'**What you see.**'"

"Do you have a comment, Kristy?"

## CHAPTER 4: PUNCTUATING CLAUSES

"Yeah, it's like 'Running across LBJ…'"

"Very good point."

By the way, let me give you a tip that helps me sniff out a **Noun Clause** hiding in a sentence.

*Professional Clamdigging* **Tip**

If you can replace a clause by IT or HE (or SHE, if you prefer) and it makes sense, it is a noun clause—guaranteed!

**~~What you see~~ is a painting by Monet.**
    **It**

See how that works? What word replaces the noun clause in this sentence?

Whoever finds my wallet will be a rich man.

"What's the noun clause, Giovanni?"

"'Whoever finds my wallet.'"

"That's right. Now replace it with a pronoun to prove that it is a Noun Clause."

**~~WHOEVER FINDS MY WALLET~~ will be a rich man.**
    **He**

### LESSON 8: NOUN CLAUSES — "AT YOUR SERVICE!"

Here's the memory sentence for the **Noun Clause**. Actually, it has two noun clauses. Can you find them?

*Professional Clamdigging™ Memory Sentence*

Noun Clause Memory Sentence

**What you see is what you get.**

"What are they, Kristy?"

"'What you see' and 'what you get.'"

"Good—the **Subject** and the **Predicate Noun**."

---

**Exercise 16**: Find the noun clauses in the following sentences and underline them.

1. <u>Whoever comes to the party late</u> will be out of luck.

2. I don't know what time it is.

3. <u>Whatever you want to do</u> is fine with me.

4. I'll find out where <u>he</u> is.

# CHAPTER 4: PUNCTUATING CLAUSES

5. I don't know why she hasn't called yet.

**Check answers with your cool instructor or visit lovinggrammar.com.**

---

ALL BUT ONE **noun clause** begins with a question word, so we have **one non-question word that begins a noun clause.** Can you find it in the following?

I didn't say that you were going.

"Did you find it, Kristy?"

"I think it's 'that.' But I thought that 'that' was an Adjective Clause Word."

"Uh oh! That's a problem, isn't it? Well, let's first do the Noun Clause Test on this one to make sure we know what it is."

I didn't say ~~THAT YOU WERE GOING~~.
      **It**

Okay, that's a noun clause all right. Let's compare that with an Adjective Clause Word 'that.'

1. I didn't say **that** you were going. **(Noun Clause)**

2. Never buy a truck **that** has over 200,000 miles on it. **(Adjective Clause)**

"So, Mr. Felix. We've come a long way together. Don't let me down! Do you see a difference between these two clauses? Say it like a Professional Clamdigger, please."

### LESSON 8: NOUN CLAUSES — "AT YOUR SERVICE!"

"Well, the clause in the first one answers the question WHAT. 'What' is a Noun 'move.' The clause in the second sentence answers the question WHAT KIND OF, and that is an adjective 'move.'"

"WOW! That was Professional Clamdigging™ if I've ever heard it! Kristy couldn't have said it better herself!"

"That's IT on clauses, folks! You now know as much as I do about clauses. We're done! Yes, Felix? You say there is one more clause? What is it?"

"Santa Claus!"

"Okay, thank you, Felix for that impressive information! Felix, get a grip, man. It was funny but not that funny! Hey, does anyone here know CPR?"

Let's try to mix the clauses together to see if you guys are rock solid on this lesson or not.

**Exercise 17:** Underline any clause that you see. Put **N** or **ADJ** or **ADV** above it to indicate the kind of phrase it is. Then put in commas that are needed and circle them or put **NC** in front of the sentences that need no commas.

1. What you see, is a picture of my summer home.
   N

2. No, the book that I want is over there.
   N

3. Even though I've seen the movie, I don't mind seeing it again.
   ADV

4. I don't know where he is.
   NC

253

# CHAPTER 4: PUNCTUATING CLAUSES

5. He's the one, who knows the combination to the lock.
    ADJ

6. Whenever you do that, I get nervous.
    ADV  NC

7. Give whatever you think, you can afford.
    ADV

8. The paper is on top of the book, which I got for my birthday.
    ADJ

9. Would you fix that picture, that is falling?
    ADJ  NC

10. Since you were late you'll have to finish the quiz, after school.
    ADV

**See your teacher for the answers!**

---

Now comes your chance to show off all of your new writing stuff—your clauses and phrases.

> **Exercise 18:** Write me a paragraph about "The Three Little Pigs." Put the following in it:

1. A Prepositional Phrase with comma

2. A Participial Phrase

3. An Appositive Phrase

4. A Gerund Phrase

5. An Adverb Clause (with comma)

## LESSON 8: NOUN CLAUSES — "AT YOUR SERVICE!"

6. An Adjective Clause (with comma)

7. An Adjective Clause (without commas)

8. A Noun Clause

You do not need to have these specified sentence types in order, but please number them wherever they are (using the numbers in the list above) so I can check them.

Give your story to your favorite English teacher when you are done!

CHAPTER 4: PUNCTUATING CLAUSES

# Lesson 9: ATTENTION! Final Review of Clauses

**Exercise 19**: Underline the clauses or phrases below. If it is a **clause**, put **ADV** or **ADJ** or **N** above the clause to identify it. If it is a **phrase**, put **PPs** (prep phrases), **Part** (participial), **Ger** (Gerund), or **App** (Appositive) above the phrase to identify it. Then put in necessary commas and circle the comma. If no comma is needed, put **NC** in front of the sentence.

1. After lunch on Saturday I'm leaving for Boston.

2. Screaming like a maniac Mr. Lund returned the essays to our Advanced Composition class.

3. If you're going I'm going too.

4. Whenever you're going is fine with me.

5. Whenever you visit Dallas give me a call.

6. The car that my mother has is a Honda.

7. The Ferrari which is made in Italy is my favorite car. (Hint: This car is only manufactured in one country.)

8. Complaining in a whiny voice is not a good way to communicate with me.

9. Jenny the class brain is coming over tonight to help me with my homework.

10. Since you're coming over tonight you may as well bring the book.

11. I don't know who you are anymore.

# LESSON 9: ATTENTION! FINAL REVIEW OF CLAUSES

12. Sra. Roldan who is a native of Ohio is our Spanish teacher.

13. That's the house that I was telling you about.

14. I didn't know that you were going to the prom with her.

15. This pizza which is from Uno's is the best in Dallas.

16. I wouldn't go with him if he picked me up in a Lamborghini.

17. What you did is wrong.

18. Even though I studied I bombed the test.

19. What you see is the most beautiful woman in Dallas.

20. Never buy cars that have over 160,000 miles on them.

**(Goodbye to Santa and all the Clauses.)**
**Ho, ho, ho, ho, ho, ho, ho, ho, ho, ho, ho, ho, ho, ho, ho, ho, ho, ho, ho, ho!**
**Shh! Listen to the sound of the sleigh bells in the distance: clause, clause, clause, clause, clause, clause, clause.**

CHAPTER 4: PUNCTUATING CLAUSES

# Lesson 10: Final Review

*Are you STILL REALLY with me?????????????????????????*

1. What is the definition of a Clause?

2. How many kinds of clauses are there in English? Name them.

3. What are two reasons for learning clauses?

4. List the Adverb Clause Words (subordinating conjunctions).

5. What is the Adverb Clause Mastery Rule?

# LESSON 10: FINAL REVIEW

6. What are the 6 questions an Adverb Clause can answer?

7. What is the Adverb Clause Memory Sentence?

8. What is the Adverb Clause Completeness Rule?

9. What are the four most common words that introduce an Adjective Clause?

10. What is another term for an Adjective Clause?

11. When do we use who and when do we use whom in a sentence?

# CHAPTER 4: PUNCTUATING CLAUSES

12. What are three less common adjective clause words?

13. What is a Restrictive Adjective Clause?

14. What are the Restrictive and the Non-Restrictive Adjective Clause Memory Sentences?

15. What is the Mastery Rule for punctuating Restrictive and Non-Restrictive Adjective Clauses?

16. What are two Professional Clamdigging™ tips for distinguishing restrictive and non-restrictive adjective clauses?

LESSON 10: FINAL REVIEW

17. How can commas change the meaning of a sentence?   Give an example of this.

18. What is the Noun Clause Mastery Rule?

19. Where can we find a Noun Clause in a sentence?

20. What is a tip for spotting a noun clause?

21. What is the Noun Clause Memory Sentence?

CHAPTER 5

# Mickey Mouse, Semi-Colons, and End Game Music

## Lesson 1: Introducers

Okay, my fine, feathered, flibovian Clamdigger friends! As usual, I suppose you think you're all done with grammar, and, as usual, you are dead wrong! We have just a few more short lessons before you are firmly ensconced in the bliss of Professional Clamdiggingdom although I have to admit that this will seem like Mickey Mouse stuff compared to the material you have studied, and, I hope, mastered. (Do you see the commas there at the end of that last sentence? Hmmmmm, very interesting!)

Before we get on with the show, I want to pause here on a New York dime and ask you Clamdiggers how you're doing. And don't just tell me what you think I want to hear! What's been the hardest thing for you to figure out in this grammar book so far? Go ahead and write the things that you're struggling with the most. Any nice discoveries along the way?

Write your thoughts here:

*Phrases*

## LESSON 1: INTRODUCERS

"Can we talk about it for a few minutes? Felix, how about you? What are you hating or loving about this grammar stuff?"

"Well, I like the **memory sentences**. I've never been able to remember what a gerund is or what a participial phrase is, but now because of the memory sentences and the **mastery tests**, I know exactly what they are. I like that. The hardest part for me has been the restrictive and non-restrictive adjective clauses. They are pretty tough. But putting a hand over one side of that pie chart helped me to see what restrictive means for the first time. It's cool to think that language can do that. A different clause can put you on this side or that side."

"That's great! You're on the Clamdigging Bus—and on the road to Damascus, eh? Giovanni, how about you?"

"I like the **Magical Wheel of Function**. I never thought about grammar being that simple, in a way—everything on one page—and just four moves like in chess! The hardest part for me is confusing the gerunds and the present participials, but Felix is right: the **memory sentences** are stuck in my head now, and I can compare the sentences on the exams to them, and I'm kind of surprised to see that I know what's going on. I never had any idea where to put commas."

"Kristy, has anything gotten on your radar?"

"I like the little tricks that you've taught, like the commas between coordinate adjectives—putting an 'and' between the adjectives to see if they need a comma. But I really want to know more about this 'Jazz Writing' that you're talking about."

"That's the next book, Kristy. Stick around for that. It'll be a lot fun. First, we need to make sure that we can sling around decent sentences that do what they are supposed to do. Then we can start to dress them up with 'Jazz and the other Juice.' That's my working title for the book. But really it's all **Professional Clamdigging**™—getting people to pay attention to your writing. Thanks for your input, everybody. Let's get back to work on the grammar. This is the home stretch!"

"The first thing we are going to do in this chapter is a simplification of all these comma rules—pulling them all together. Second, we're going to figure out how to use the semi-colon."

---

### Introducer comma rules

---

"In case you haven't noticed by now, we English-speaking peoples like to use commas in two main ways. The first is separating out elements that serve as introducers to a sentence. The second is…yes, Felix?"

"I think I know what it is."

"You're starting to remind me of Kristy. Is that what this world has come to? What do you think is the second way, Felix?"

"Never mind."

"Oh, oh. I hope I didn't hurt your feelings, Felix! Believe it or not, I was trying to give you a compliment. The truth is that you've already *shown* us the second reason for commas—**interrupters**, so don't worry. You'll get your piece of the watermelon, buddy. *Nobody* interrupts like you do. If you want to see what I mean, go back to the first page of this book. And, let's face it: **life would be much less interesting, Felix, without interruptions, as you will see in the next lesson.**"

"Okay, let's start at the beginning before I forget what I want to accomplish. These are the Introducers that we have studied so far in this book."

# LESSON 1: INTRODUCERS

**Introducers (Please write the name of the mastery rule over the comma in each sentence.)**

1. In my room under my bed **(COMMA),** you'll find my Geometry book.

2. Insulted by the tone of his voice **(COMMA),** she hit the end button on her cell phone.

3. Smiling like a Cheshire cat **(COMMA),** she slammed the door in my face.

4. Whenever I see an adverb clause at the beginning of a sentence **(COMMA),** I put a comma right after it.

5. To punctuate correctly **(COMMA),** you need to know quite a bit of grammar.

These are the **introducers** you already know that take commas.

"Kristy, can you tell us what grammar you found in those sentences?"

1. **Introductory prepositional phrase**

2. **Introductory past participial phrase**

3. **Introductory present participial phrase**

4. **Introductory adverb clause**

5. **Introductory infinitive phrase**

## MICKEY MOUSE, SEMI-COLONS, AND END GAME MUSIC

"You get the picture? These rules are all the same, in a way. Yes, Kristy?"

> "You mean as I get older like you, Mr. Lund, and start forgetting what the grammatical structure is, I can say it needs a comma because it's an introductory 'something' or other."

"Wellllllll, uhhhhhhhhhhhhh, I guess you could do worse than that, Kristy, if you lose your tattered and torn copy of **Clamdigging**."

"In any case, those are the hard introducers. Now come the easy ones. Ready, everyone? Can I get a drum roll, Mr. Giovanni? Ta da da DA! The MICKEY MOUSERS!!!"

### Professional Clamdigging™ Mastery Rule:

**The Mickey Mouse Comma Rule**

Put a comma after 'yes,' 'no,' or any 'noise' words that come at the beginning of the sentence.

LESSON 1: INTRODUCERS

# Professional Clamdigging™ Memory Sentence

## The Mickey Mouse Comma Memory Sentence:

### Hey, leave me alone!

**Exercise 1**: Put commas in the following sentences and make a note of those 'noise words':

1. Look, I'm not going to put up with any more of this abuse from you.

2. No, there's no mail today.

3. Well, I'll take the garbage out if you give your brother a bath.

4. Ah, it's great to be back in the USA!

5. Hey, turn that music down, will you, please?

6. So, I think it's time to have a little talk about responsibilities around here.

7. Yes, I'm going to the game with you.

8. Of course, I would prefer to see the game live, wouldn't you?

9. Okay, count me in.

## MICKEY MOUSE, SEMI-COLONS, AND END GAME MUSIC

10. Look, this is the day that we agreed to get this stuff done.

So all introducers (whether one word or twenty words) look like this in a sentence:

**Introducer (COMMA),** the rest of the sentence.

# Professional Clamdigging™ Mastery Rule:

### Introducer Mastery Comma Rule

Put a comma after participial phrases, multiple prepositional phrases, infinitive phrases, adverb clauses, and Mickey Mouse introducers that come at the beginning of a sentence.

**Exercise 2:** Write out eight sentences using this comma rule. Use the kind of noise words that are common in your speech at home and at school.

1. Ahwhah, I'm falling.

LESSON 1: INTRODUCERS

2. Ho Ho, Thats an owl.

3. Brumm, You want to race.

4. Crunch, this cookies is delishis.

5. mmm, I love food.

6. Yee ha, I'm a cowboy.

7. Bang, lightning just struk that tree.

8. Pew Pew, Go into lightspeed chewe.

**Please turn in your sentences to your teacher when you are finished!**

MICKEY MOUSE, SEMI-COLONS, AND END GAME MUSIC

# Lesson 2: Interrupters

Next up, the more—how shall I say this?—reserved and modest **Interrupters**. (And by the way, please interrupt me, Felix, whenever you have a question.)

**Interrupter Commas** (once again, please identify the grammar rule involved in each— write it above the comma).

1. Mr. Lund **(COMMA),** my Clamdigging teacher **(COMMA),** comes from Chicago.

2. My girlfriend **(COMMA),** smiling like a Cheshire Cat **(COMMA),** slammed the door in my face.

3. My truck **(COMMA),** which is a Nissan **(COMMA),** has 60,000 miles on it.

Here's what these interrupters look like:

**The beginning of the sentence (COMMA), interrupter (COMMA),** end of the sentence.

"So what grammar issues did you write down for these sentences, Giovanni?"

1. Appositive
2. Present Participle
3. Non-Restrictive Adjective Clause

"These structures are called interrupters because, like most high school students in English class (heh, heh), they **INTERRUPT THE MAIN AGENDA**."

# LESSON 2: INTERRUPTERS

"And the good news is that you've already learned the hard interrupters. That's what you see up there in Giovanni's answers. Now get ready to meet…"

## THE EASY INTERRUPTERS.

**Parenthetical Expressions: (always set off with commas)!**

, I believe (or think, know, hope, etc.),
, I am sure,
, on the other hand,
, on the contrary,
, after all,
, by the way,
, incidentally,
, in fact,
, indeed,
, of course,
, for example,

- Geometry, for example, is infinitely more interesting than Algebra I.

Notice this expression can be moved to other parts of the sentence, and notice how this changes the use of commas. Circle the commas while you're at it.

- For example, Geometry is infinitely more interesting than Algebra I.

- Geometry is infinitely more interesting than Algebra I, for example.

- Geometry, for example, is infinitely more interesting than Algebra I.

## MICKEY MOUSE, SEMI-COLONS, AND END GAME MUSIC

I hope, by the way, you see that these three sentence are not exactly the same, but the differences are stylistic, an issue that you will learn a lot more about in the next Professional Clamdigging™ book on *Writing Jazz*.

"Yes, Felix?"

"You said interrupt you, so I'm interrupting you."

"Okay, what's on your mind?"

"What's your favorite TV show, Mr. Lund?"

"We're going to stop Clamdigging to talk about TV? Besides, you don't want to know my favorite TV show."

"Yeah, we do."

"Stay out of this, Kristy. Okay, okay. I'll tell you. You've probably never even heard of this show—it's as old as the hills. It's called *Everybody Loves Raymond*. I like it because Raymond's wife, Debra reminds me of my wife. If something upsets her at a party or some place, she stays quiet and sweet until the car ride home—then comes the explosion. I like the jazz soundtrack in that show too."

"Does that answer your question, Felix? Now aren't you sorry you used up your interrupter card for that? Let's do an exercise."

**LESSON 2: INTERRUPTERS**

**Exercise 3**: Write out seven sentences using the parenthetical expressions. Make your sentences kind of funny, and put the interrupters in various positions of the sentence.

1. Mrs. Perry, my math teacher, likes chineses food.

2. When I drive, my loud cars, it's fun.

3. I love to eat, snaks, because it satisfiys me.

4. My dog, smiling like a cheshire cat, is so cute.

5. My TV, which is a samsung, is to best

6. My house, which is tiny, is so cozey.

7. My brother, who is nice, always mess with me.

## Professional Clamdigging™ Mastery Rule:

### Interrupter Mastery Comma Rule

Set off with commas parenthetical expressions, persons addressed, appositive phrases, participial phrases, and adjective phrases that interrupt the main part of a sentence.

### Professional Clamdigging™ Memory Sentence
Interrupter Mastery Comma Rule

Go ahead and interrupt me, Felix, whenever you want!

**LESSON 2: INTERRUPTERS**

"Wow, I get a memory sentence dedicated to me? Thanks, Mr. Lund!"

"You're welcome, my friend. That's for putting up with all my corny jokes. One more exercise and then I'll have something to say that you are all definitely going to want to hear! And I guarantee it!"

**Exercise 4:** Put in commas that are needed and circle the commas.

1. Randy, did you remember to pack my swim suit?

2. Hey, look at that.

3. Tomorrow, I hope, is our last Clamdigger lesson.

4. Mabel, incidentally, is no longer my steady girlfriend.

5. Tuesday, in fact, is another dress-up day at school.

6. No, I can't come over this weekend.

7. Oh, you're from Chicago too?

8. On the contrary, I love to jog in the morning.

9. I just got back, by the way, from my High School Reunion in Chicago.

10. Hey, I saw a great movie about "Soul Music" on the plane ride home.

**Check answers with the big boss please!**

## MICKEY MOUSE, SEMI-COLONS, AND END GAME MUSIC

"What movie did you see, Mr. Lund?"

"It's called 'The Sapphires,' Kristy. It's about some young Australian black women singers that learn 'Soul' music from a white Irish dude and then take it on tour to the Vietnam War. It is absolutely almost as good as Lars*. And apparently, it really happened! It's got great Motown 'Soul Music' from the 60s and it's very funny too—imagine a white dude teaching black women how to sing 'black.' And he does it too!"

*Lars and the Real Girl*

"Let's get back to business, Clamdiggers. And now (ahem) it gives me great pleasure to make an earth-shattering announcement. Here it is:

**"Folks, thaaaaaaaaaaaaaaaaaaaaaat's IT on commas!"**

"You can't be serious. Finally, it's over? I'm going to tell my grandchildren about this moment."

"Very funny, Giovanni. I'll dream up a few more if you like. Seriously, you guys have been around long enough to know that there are a few other comma possibilities in things like addresses and dates and dialogue, right? (That's another comma opportunity for you—the tag questions, like the one at the end of the last sentence.) I'm guessing that you have been working with these for a long time, and I don't think they involve the same grammatical complexities that we have faced up to in this book. So, I'm confident that you can handle those on your own. Kristy? Now what did I do wrong?"

"Can we celebrate a little?"

"Okay then—let's celebrate this stellar occasion by doing the Watusi, and then we'll do a little review quiz. Let's cue a little music on YouTube—what do you say? How about 'Hold on, I'm Coming,' either by Sam and Dave or by the Blues Brothers—or both! There you go—there's some 'Soul Music' for you."

## LESSON 2: INTERRUPTERS

"Go ahead stand up and Watusi first. Go wild! What do you mean you don't know how to Watusi? Watusi?? Are you serious? We did this back in chapter 2—the James Brown chapter, didn't we? C'mon, Kristy: show us how it's done."

"Sorry, Mr. Lund. I don't remember anything about the Watusi!"

"I'm going to have to include a review on dances in the next edition of this book, I suppose. The final exam will be to dance to Wilson Pickett's 'Land of 1000 Dances.'"

**Well that's all for today, folks—Watusi or no Watusi!**

MICKEY MOUSE, SEMI-COLONS, AND END GAME MUSIC

# Lesson 3: More Sick Sentences: Fragments, Run-ons, and Comma Splices

Okay, before we get to our next and last grammar and punctuation problem, my friends, the mere mention of which, by the way, will strike dread terror into your heart, let's do a nice mastery exercise on all comma rules.

One last little warning: this exercise includes some of those other Mickey Mouse commas rules that you should know since 7th grade (probably more like 5th grade): you know, dates and addresses, comma and conjunction to join independent clauses, that kind of thing.

> "Wait? What's that 'comma and conjunction to join independent clauses,' Mr. Lund?"

"Watch this, Felix. I'm going to perform some magic! Watch carefully!"

**Sentence 1:** I'm studying Professional Clamdigging with a guy named Mr. Lund.

**Sentence 2:** I think I'm finally starting to get this comma stuff.

**Sentence 1 and 2 combined:**                    **comma, conjunction**
I'm studying Professional Clamdigging with a guy named Mr. Lund**, and** I think I'm finally starting to get this comma stuff.

"Got it, my friend?"

> "Got it. Thanks, Mr. Lund."

**LESSON 3: MORE SICK SENTENCES**

**Exercise 5:** Put commas in the following where they are needed and circle the commas. If no commas are necessary, put NC in front of the sentence or phrase.

1. Jazz music, which is a beautiful and unique American art form, needs to be studied and preserved.

2. Jan, my older sister, ran over to the store in 15 minutes.

3. Even though she was tired, she ran back.

4. She looked for bread, but there wasn't any left.

NC 5. I don't know who you're talking about.

6. I don't like spinach, and I don't like couscous.

NC 7. She's the CPA who did my taxes.

8. After you finish the exam, you can put it on my desk.

NC 9. I don't like liver or kidneys.

10. Before lunch, I went to the post office.

NC 11. I never see movies when they first come out.

12. On September 11, 2001, America was cruelly attacked in New York.

13. I worked at Dallas Lutheran School, 8494 Stults Road, Dallas, Texas, until May 2013.

NC 14. Sincerely yours

## MICKEY MOUSE, SEMI-COLONS, AND END GAME MUSIC

15. Walter G. Prausnitz, PhD.

16. William Kendall, Jr.

17. Her messy, greasy hair was shoved into a scarf.

18. Whenever she looks at me, like that, I feel helpless.

19. I don't know, as a matter of fact, where you live.

20. After the play, we'll be going over to Brent's house.

21. If you come without your homework, you will be marked absent.

22. Charging through the door, she slammed her books down on the desk and took her seat.

23. I'm not going to the game, and they're not going either.

24. I'll bring the chips, the dip, the hot sauce, and the guacamole.

25. John, my sister's best friend, is from Kentucky.

26. That restaurant, which opened in 2002, is excellent.

27. A truck, with over 260,000 miles on it, should probably be traded.

28. Yes, I'll be there tonight.

29. I'm taking Karen to the dance, Aaron.

LESSON 3: MORE SICK SENTENCES

30. After school, I'm going shopping, fixing my car, and picking my coat up at the cleaners.

31. Trapped on the sandbar, the amateur clamdiggers had to send a text for help.

**Check your answers with the teacher.**

---

Now that we are finished with phrases and clauses, I'd like to give you one final check-up on writing healthy sentences and fixing sick ones.

# Professional Clamdigging™ Mastery Rule:

### Healthy (Complete) Sentence Mastery Rule

A healthy (complete) sentence must have all its parts (dependent and independent), and it must have a period when it is finished.

# MICKEY MOUSE, SEMI-COLONS, AND END GAME MUSIC

## ADVERB CLAUSE FRAGMENTS

Now let's look at some of the diseases that afflict English sentences. Probably the #1 sentence health hazard is the **sentence fragment.** We have already seen some of these when we studied dependent (adverb) clauses.

*Whenever she looks at me like that with cold eyes and tight lips.

*Remember, the asterisk tells us that something is wrong in the sentence.

"Can you fix that one, Giovanni? And, by the way, what's the matter with it?"

"Well, it's a dependent adverb clause that needs the independent clause."

Whenever she looks at me like that with cold eyes and tight lips, I start checking my phone for updates.

"Well, I doubt that that's going to fix things up between you and your lady, Giovanni, but you did fix the fragment."

## ADJECTIVE CLAUSE FRAGMENT

In some cases the fragment may not be an adverb clause. It may be another clause.

Underline the fragment in the following:

*I saw her yesterday in that new outfit. Which must have cost a fortune.

## LESSON 3: MORE SICK SENTENCES

"Kristy, what do we do with this mess?"

"Well, the first part is fine, but the second part is a fragment. I would combine the two."

"What do you call that second part, Kristy?"

"It's an adjective clause."

"Keep going."

"It's non-restrictive, which means that we need commas."

"Be my guest, Kristy."

I saw her yesterday in that new outfit, which must have cost a fortune.

---

### PHRASE FRAGMENT

---

*We got there too late to see my aunt. Her plane having left at 2:00.

"Felix, you're on deck for the next one."

"Okay. I think you can just connect them together."

We got there too late to see my aunt, her plane having left at 2:00.

"Here's another sick puppy for you to fix, Giovanni."

I saw her yesterday. Going to her third period class.

## MICKEY MOUSE, SEMI-COLONS, AND END GAME MUSIC

"That's easy. Just make them one sentence."

I saw her yesterday going to her third period class.

**Exercise 6**: Do whatever you need to do to fix the following sentences that do not feel well.

1. My best friend, having come all the way from Chile to see me,
   _____
   _____

2. While shopping yesterday in the frozen goods department at Tom Thumb, which is way at the back of the store.
   _____
   _____

3. Because you never clean your room when I ask you to.
   _____
   _____

4. If she would choose to either call us from the airport or to call, collect from the hotel.
   _____
   _____

5. Dr. Prausnitz, having been educated at the University of Chicago, an institution famous for its graduate programs in the Humanities.
   _____
   _____

---

"Aren't those lovely creatures? Now you know why English teachers lose so much hair every year. It's not the vitamin deficiency, my friends!"

Before we go on to the other type of sick sentences, let me point out a fact to you. English teachers and all intelligent readers are greatly offended by the three kinds of sick sen-

## LESSON 3: MORE SICK SENTENCES

tences you are studying in this unit (**fragments, run-ons and comma splices**). Some teachers have been known to rip papers containing sick sentences into tiny fragments—I know, don't say it: thereby creating even more sentence fragments—heh, heh. I even saw one teacher eating these paper fragments when the shredding process was not enough to assuage him.

Now admittedly that is a rather extreme reaction, but more limited responses are common too. As for me, I take off three points out of a possible 100 for each sick sentence I find in a student essay. As you can imagine, this can have a fairly devastating impact on your grade.

"Why *do* teachers get so bent out shape over fragments, Mr. Lund?"

"Let me try to show you, Felix. I'll give you three sentences with writing errors, and you put a second star in front of the one that is hardest to understand."

1. *There he was in the backsit of the car.

2. * Hey, my friend, Bill don't care if you've studied judo for 1400 year.

3. *Having called her up on the phone 30 times per day for the last week with no success whatsoever.

"Well, Felix?"

"I'm going to have to go with sentence #3."

"And your reasoning?"

"I can figure out the meaning of the other sentences. With number three you are lost in trying to understand it."

## MICKEY MOUSE, SEMI-COLONS, AND END GAME MUSIC

"Can you finish it so that it makes sense, Felix?"

> Having called her up on the phone 30 times per day for the last week with no success whatsoever, he decided that she didn't want to talk to him.

"I think you diagnosed the content and the structure of that sentence perfectly, Mr. Happy-man!"

Okay, the second group of sick sentences goes by two names, although, as you will see, they really are about the same—one has a comma, one doesn't—both are wrong!

**RUN-ONS** (doesn't have a comma) AND **COMMA SPLICES** (has a comma)

**Run-on sentence:** *We love music we are going to a concert tomorrow night.

**Comma splice:** *We love music, we are going to a concert tomorrow night.

"What do these two sentences have in common, Kristy?"

> "They are really two sentences, and so you can't just put them together without a period. If you put them together with a comma, they are called a **COMMA SPLICE**; if you just run them together with no punctuation, they are a **RUN-ON**!"

"That's right. These sentences violate our healthy sentence mastery rule because they do not contain a period when the sentence is finished, or a semi-colon* when an independent clause is finished."

*Semi-colons are coming up next, by the way.

What do we do to fix a run-on or a comma splice?

LESSON 3: MORE SICK SENTENCES

**Professional Clamdigging Tip**

Use a period and capital letter between the independent clauses.

**We love music. We're going to a concert tomorrow night.**

**Professional Clamdigging Tip**

Use a semi-colon between the independent clauses.

**We love music; we're going to a concert tomorrow night.**

MICKEY MOUSE, SEMI-COLONS, AND END GAME MUSIC

### Professional Clamdigging Tip

Use a conjunction (and, but, or) and a COMMA after the first independent clause.

**We love classical music, and we're going to a concert tomorrow night.**

**Exercise 7:** Now please rewrite the following paragraph, fixing all the sick sentences that you see. Look for fragments, run-on sentences and comma splices.

Have you ever wondered what would happen if you drove away from a gas station with the gas nozzle still in your car? Which happened to me, one day I got gas. While waiting for my son to get off work at a restaurant which was very embarrassing. After I got the gas. I drove over to the restaurant with the car radio on very loud. All of a sudden someone was knocking hysterically on my window. He must have been from another country, his English was not too good he said you have my "thing-ee" I got out of the car to look, he pointed to the rubber hose waving back and forth from the gas compartment, I knew what I had done I had to pay for the connector that was broken.

**Rewritten:**

*Have you ever wondered what would happen, if you drove away from a gas station with the gas nozzle still in your car? Which happened to me, one day when I got gas. While waiting for my son to get off work at a restaurant, which was very embarrassing. After I got the gas; I drove over to the restaurant with the car*

# LESSON 3: MORE SICK SENTENCES

radio very loud. All of a sudden someone was knocking hysterically on my window. He must have been from another country, his English was not to good. He said you have my, "thing-ee!" I got out of the car to look. He pointed to the rubber hose waving back and forth from the gas compartment. I knew what I had done, I had to pay for the connecter that was broken.

**Give the rewritten paragraph to your teacher when you are done.**

---

**Exercise 8**: Just to see if you remember all the **PROFESSIONAL CLAMDIGGING TIPS** I've taught you, please fix the following sick sentence in three different ways.

**\*My mother works full-time my father works part-time.**

1. My mother works full-time. My father works part-time.

2. My mother works full-time; my father works part-time.

3. My mother works full-time, and my father works part-time.

289

# MICKEY MOUSE, SEMI-COLONS, AND END GAME MUSIC

## Show the answers to your teacher, my friends!

---

"Kristy, do you have a question?"

"Is that made up about the gas station or did that happen to you, Mr. Lund?"

"I'm sorry to report that it did actually happen to me years ago when I was going through an 'absent-minded professor' phase of my life."

"How much did it cost for the nozzle connecter?"

"I think it was about $8.00. It was not nearly as bad as I thought it would be. But I will never forget the look on that guy's face when he said 'You have my thing-ee!'"

**Next up: Semi-Colons!**

# Lesson 4: Who's Afraid of Semi-colons?

"Let me take a little survey. How many of you use semi-colons regularly in your writing? I'm not seeing any hands. Did you guys not hear the question?"

"No, we heard it, but we don't use semi-colons."

"Why not—Giovanni?"

"I have no idea how to use them."

"Felix?"

"I'm scared to death of semi-colons; I really am!" (I know—don't say anything!)

"Kristy?"

"I'm not sure exactly sure when to use them? I kind of know but I'm afraid of looking like a fool if I screw it up."

"Look, we're all friends by now and we've been through a lot together. We know that we can get through this stuff. And I never thought I would hear that Kristy is afraid of looking like a fool. May I tell you something about semi-colons? **Semi-colons are the Lamborghinis of punctuation**. If you park a Lamborghini in front of a sidewalk restaurant, everyone will sit up and take notice. If you correctly use a semi-colon, everybody will know that you are a **Professional Clamdigger**!

"So, let's figure this out. I want everybody to get it—as usual! The first thing you need to do is memorize the **Semi-Colon Words**. These are great words, and I don't think you've seen them before in *Loving Grammar: Mr. Lund's Guide to Professional Clamdigging*™. If you want to know what the technical word is for these, keep reading until the end of the paragraph. If your skin crawls at the sound of technical-sounding grammar terms,

## MICKEY MOUSE, SEMI-COLONS, AND END GAME MUSIC

jump down to the list of semi-colon words which has been previewed for non-professional Clamdigging audiences."

"Very funny! We can handle it, Mr. Lund."

"Good for you, Giovanni. These semi-colon words are also known as **conjunctive adverbs**."

Here's the list: Would you do me a favor? Circle the semi-colon before and the commas and after the words below. Thank you.

**SEMI-COLON WORDS** (Memorize these for class tomorrow!)

;however,
;instead,
;nevertheless,
;therefore,
;consequently,
;furthermore,
;moreover,

LESSON 4: WHO'S AFRAID OF SEMI-COLONS?

# Professional Clamdigging™ Mastery Rule:

## The Semi-Colon Mastery Rule

Whenever you see a "semi-colon word" in a sentence between two independent clauses, put a semi-colon in front of the "semi-colon word" and a comma right after it – like this:

## Professional Clamdigging™ Memory Sentence

The Semi-Colon Memory Sentence

I am a pretty good writer; however, I always have trouble getting started.

## MICKEY MOUSE, SEMI-COLONS, AND END GAME MUSIC

**Exercise 9**: Now punctuate the following sentences using the semi-colon rule. Remember, put a semi-colon before the word and a comma after it.

1. I didn't go to the conference; instead, I went to see a new Woody Allen movie.

2. You are not careful with your organization and your punctuation; furthermore, you have been late with every one of your essays.

3. I decided that I would talk to him about it the next day; however, I changed my mind as soon as I woke up.

4. You have been an outstanding and a diligent Spanish student; consequently, you have been chosen to be the recipient of the 1990 Bravo Ramiro Award.

5. I am a great fan of the Cubs; nevertheless, I'm hoping that Pittsburgh goes to the World Series.

6. You refused to give me a refund for the damaged merchandise; moreover, you refused to let me exchange the damaged one for a good one.

7. We've decided to cancel our subscriptions to cable TV; therefore, we will no longer be able to watch Chicago Cubs baseball games.

---

## HOLD THE PHONE, GUYS; WE'RE NOT DONE WITH SEMI-COLONS!

"The **second way to use semi-colons** is to use it between two independent clauses that are closely related to each other. Look at the sentence above. What is the first clause, Giovanni?"

LESSON 4: WHO'S AFRAID OF SEMI-COLONS?

"Hold the phone, guys."

"Is that an independent clause? Could it stand by itself as a sentence?"

"Yes."

"How about the second clause? Is that dependent or independent?"

"It's independent too."

"So, notice that we can put a semi-colon between two independent clauses without any other connector."

---

Independent Clause      Semi-colon      Independent Clause

**HOLD THE PHONE, GUYS; WE'RE NOT DONE WITH SEMI-COLONS! (part 2)**

But remember, we should only do this when the sentences are closely related.

"What do you mean 'closely related,' Mr. Lund?"

"Well, when one sentence is really extended or completed by the next one, we would say that they are closely related to each other. Here are some examples.

Today is February 18th; it's my birthday. (Closely related)

My favorite teacher in college was Dr. Prausnitz. He grew up in Germany before World War II. (Not as closely related).

---

# MICKEY MOUSE, SEMI-COLONS, AND END GAME MUSIC

**Exercise 10**: Put semi-colons between the independent clauses that are closely related to each other.

1. I had lunch with Jerry today; We ate at the Flying Fish in Dallas.

2. My wife is from Indiana; I met her fifteen years ago.

3. I'm sick today; I'm feverish.

4. Tomorrow is the big game; We have to win it!

5. Last week I talked to Gerry Kosinski, a very close friend of mine, who is in hospice; We talked about his favorite band, Pink Floyd.

---

"Mr. Lund? Could we go over these together? I'm having trouble with these. And what does 'hospice' mean?"

Sure, Felix. And don't worry. There is no hard and fast line that determines whether we should use a period or a semi-colon between two independent clauses. I'm just trying to help you see the purpose of choosing a semi-colon rather than the usual—a period—to connect two independent clauses. 'Hospice' is a kind of hospital or care facility for people who are dying."

"Now, do you see any sentences in this exercise that complete each other or are very closely related?"

"I think that sentence 3 maybe should have a semi-colon because those two clauses are really just adding information to each other."

"Very good, Felix. I agree with you. Are there any others? Giovanni?"

### LESSON 4: WHO'S AFRAID OF SEMI-COLONS?

"How about number 2?"

"Kristy, do you have a comment?"

"Yeah, I don't think those are that closely related. The first one talks about where you met your wife and the second part is about how long ago that was. I think number 4 should get a semi-colon because all that matters about the game is that we need to win it and that makes it a big game."

I think that's a good point. So let's look at the sentences in Exercise 10 with the punctuation that we've discussed.

1. I had lunch with Jerry today. We ate at the Flying Fish in Dallas.

2. My wife is from Indiana. I met her fifteen years ago.

3. I'm sick today; I'm feverish. **(semi-colon)**

4. Tomorrow is the big game; we have to win it! **(semi-colon)**

5. Last week I talked to Gerry Kosinski, a very close friend of mine, who is in hospice. We talked about his favorite band, Pink Floyd.

(Please note that when we join two independent clauses together with a semi-colon we do NOT start the second clause with a capital letter unless the first word is already capitalized by itself, like the word 'I' in number 3.)

---

## HOLD THE PHONE, GUYS; WE'RE NOT DONE WITH SEMI-COLONS! (part 3)

Now I don't know how to tell you this because it's going to make you mad at me, and you know how much I hate it when you get mad at little ol' me—but there are some times when you **DON'T** use semi-colons with Semi-Colon Words. **This is the third and last**

## MICKEY MOUSE, SEMI-COLONS, AND END GAME MUSIC

**thing that we will do with semi-colons!**

Look at the following two sentences.

**In one sentence you use commas and a semi-colon; in the other sentence you only use commas.**

A. John, however, is playing for the Eagles.

B. John is playing for the Eagles; however, his brother is cheering for the Cowboys.

Can you tell me why you punctuated them like you did? Uh, I'm seeing a lot of blank looks. Let's take another look at the semi-colon mastery rule and memory sentence.

# Professional Clamdigging™ Mastery Rule:

### The Semi-Colon Mastery Rule

Whenever you see a "semi-colon word" in a sentence between two independent clauses, put a semi-colon in front of the "semi-colon word" and a comma right after it – like this:

LESSON 4: WHO'S AFRAID OF SEMI-COLONS?

# Professional Clamdigging™ Memory Sentence
## The Semi-Colon Memory Sentence

> I am a pretty good writer; however, I always have trouble getting started.

"Giovanni, do you see what's going on?"

"I think so. Sentence B has two clauses."

"What are the clauses, G-man?"

"'John is playing for the Eagles' is the first one. 'His brother is cheering for the Cowboys' is the second one. So they are joined by the semi-colon word. But in sentence A, 'however' is between two parts of one independent clause, isn't it?"

"That's exactly right. Good work, Giovanni!"

    Subj         Verb

**A. John, however, is playing for the Eagles.** (**one** independent clause)

"So what role is 'however' playing now in this sentence, Giovanni?"

"I'm not sure what you mean."

"I think I know, Mr. Lund."

## MICKEY MOUSE, SEMI-COLONS, AND END GAME MUSIC

"Okay, Kristy. What is it?"

"It's like an **interrupter**, which needs to be set off with commas."

"Exactly right. **So if the Semi-Colon Word joins two independent clauses together, it needs a semi-colon and a comma after it**—as it says in the Semi-Colon Mastery Rule. But **if it comes in the middle of one independent clause**, then it is acting like an interrupter and needs to be punctuated like an **interrupter**—commas before and after it."

"Good job, Kristy, and good job, Giovanni. You see, we really need to think about what's going on in the sentence to know how to punctuate it. Let's practice these now.

---

**Exercise 11**: Punctuate the following sentences and be sure to circle any commas or semi-colons that you use.

1. Wearing his Cub Scout uniform and his paratrooper boots, my son marched up Laramie Avenue to his elementary school.

2. Our football team has all fifteen returning seniors; therefore we stand a good chance of winning District competition.

3. My aunt's taste in dessert selections, moreover has not changed in 25 years.

4. Kelly wanted me to help in painting the bedroom; nevertheless she allowed me to go to the Beethoven concert with Dailey.

5. My appointment with Attila's mom, however was not the end of my problems that day.

## LESSON 4: WHO'S AFRAID OF SEMI-COLONS?

6. I've never been a great fan of blue-grass music; nevertheless I really enjoyed that fiddler we saw today.

7. I spent all day in the postmaster's office; however I never got to see him.

8. The struggle for equality in pay has been a central issue in the Women's Movement; moreover that struggle continues to this day.

**Check answers with your teacher as soon as you can!**

---

"I just got a great idea: let's tell the story of the guys in the Clamdigger sentence. Everybody gets a turn and everybody HAS to do one thing: use a semi-colon in your part of the story."

"How about getting us started, Giovanni? You do remember THE sentence, don't you?"

> "Yeah. Okay, here goes. Two amateur clamdiggers, Pete and Don went to the beach this past weekend. They loved digging for clams; however, they were not familiar with tides and found themselves in deep water."

"Very good. Kristy, what happens in Act 2?"

> "This was not good. Pete and Don were in rising, cold water that soon would be over their heads; they could not swim. What could they do?"

"Felix, it's up to you to bring them on home!"

> "Two F-16 jets flew by very fast; nevertheless, one of the pilots happened to notice that Pete and Don were waving their arms in distress. He radioed to a friend of his, who called Batman, but Batman could not swim; instead, he called Superman, who

swooped in and rescued the boys."

"Now it's your turn, Mr. Lund."

"The story was all over the evening news; consequently, by morning, Pete and Don had received hundreds of supportive text messages and 6,000 kids had 'friended' them on Facebook. Now they are getting ready to start shooting a pilot episode of a reality show about clamdigging and punctuation."

"That was cool! Hey, maybe we should make a movie of this book!"

"You know what, Felix? That would be fun! Who would we get to play you?"

"I know!"

"Wait, wait, wait. Before we start shooting any movies, we'd better finish the job we started in this book. We have one more thing left to do before we are done with this journey. Felix, I want you to punctuate that Clamdigging sentence. Can you do that? Here it is for everyone to see."

**(Put commas in this sentence.)**

Trapped on a sand bar by the incoming tide the amateur clamdiggers Pete and Don who could not swim had to be rescued.

"Are you ready, sir? Don't be nervous or you'll be executed on the spot! And when you put in a comma, tell us why you are doing it, okay?"

"Okay. 'Trapped on a sand bar by the incoming tide' is a participial phrase, so we need to put a comma after that."

LESSON 4: WHO'S AFRAID OF SEMI-COLONS?

"Past or present?"

"Past."

"Okay, what's next?"

"Put a comma after Pete and Don. That is an appositive phrase."

"Bingo-palooza! Now for the whole enchilada—and the whole watermelon! Keep your eyes on the prize!"

"Put a comma after 'swim.' 'Who could not swim' is an adjective clause."

"Restrictive or non-restrictive? Careful!"

"Non-restrictive—so we need to set it off with a comma."

"I've got a question about that. How do you know that it is non-restrictive, Felix?"

"We have their names, so everything is non-restrictive after that."

**WOW!** **The Professional Clamdigging™** Bus has arrived in downtown Damascus! I am so proud of you, Felix baby! You did it! And you told me that you didn't get grammar! You are a Pro now! Here is the sentence we started the course with—now in all its punctuated glory!

## MICKEY MOUSE, SEMI-COLONS, AND END GAME MUSIC

> "Trapped on a sand bar by the incoming tide, the amateur clamdiggers, Pete and Don, who could not swim, had to be rescued."

(Warriner 535)

Time to CELEBRATE! Push the chairs back, everybody!

And, if your teacher can handle one more tune on YouTube, here it is:

"I'm a Soul Man," by Sam and Dave. Have fun, you guys! See you tomorrow!

LESSON 5: THE WORLD FAMOUS PROFESSIONAL CLAMDIGGING™ REVIEW—"THE END GAME"

# Lesson 5: The World Famous PROFESSIONAL CLAMDIGGING™ Review—"The End Game"

Are you ready to be knighted and known throughout the kingdom of the U.S.A and the world as a Professional Clamdigger™? Well, we shall see if you are ready. First, you must answer the following amateur, semi-pro, and professional clamdigging questions. This is not only an open book review, but I want you to put the page number where you found the answer.

## Part I

1. How many moves are there in grammar? What are they? How is chess like grammar?
   *4 Adjectives, Adverbs, verbs, noun*

2. What is the definition of an English sentence?
   *A group of English words that follow a pattern*

3. Why do we need to know the linking verbs in order to be Professional Clamdiggers?
   *is,*

4. What are the linking verbs?

# MICKEY MOUSE, SEMI-COLONS, AND END GAME MUSIC

5. Why do we need to know the two kinds of sentences?
   To know what to do

6. What are the three sentence possibilities for Type I sentences, and what are the three sentence possibilities for Type II sentences?

7. What is the Noun test?

8. What is the Action Verb Test? What is the Linking Verb Test?

9. What is the Adjective Test?

10. Identify the following sentences as Type I (LV) or Type II (AcV)

   1 a. We became buddies in grade school.
   2 b. I cried like a baby.
   2 c. Sra. Roldan gave us way too much homework last night!

# LESSON 5: THE WORLD FAMOUS PROFESSIONAL CLAMDIGGING™ REVIEW — "THE END GAME"

1 d. That smells terrible.
2 e. I sent her a DVD for her birthday.
2 f. Then she hit him again with the rolling pin.
2 g. She tasted the sushi slowly.
1 h. That pizza doesn't smell too great.
2 i. The buzzer sounded before the end of the game.
1 j. She stayed as calm as she could.
2 k. My brother appeared twice in the musical.
1 l. How does that salad dressing taste?
1 m. She appears to be very stubborn.

11. Which is correct: I feel (good/well).

12. Why?
    _____
    _____

13. Is there any time when the other answer could be correct? (Hint: different meaning of the word 'well.')
    _____
    _____
    _____

14. What are the irregular subject pronouns that are always singular? (There are twelve of them!)
    _____
    _____
    _____
    _____

# MICKEY MOUSE, SEMI-COLONS, AND END GAME MUSIC

15. What other nouns are always singular?

16. Which is correct and why?

   a. Each of us (plan/**plans**) to stay in the state for lower college tuition.

   b. Mr. Couser, along with one of his three sons and grandsons, (**is**/are) taking me to a NASCAR race.

   c. Either Miss Klekamp or Dr. Brunworth (**is**/are) in charge of lunch today.

   d. The whole herd of buffalo (**has**/have) contracted a rare disease.

17. What is the best way to avoid problems with each of the sentences above?

## LESSON 5: THE WORLD FAMOUS PROFESSIONAL CLAMDIGGING™ REVIEW—"THE END GAME"

18. What is the adjective function?
    _____
    _____

19. What is the adverb function?
    _____
    _____

20. Which is correct and why?

    a. That lasagna recipe sounds (delicious/deliciously).
    _____
    _____

    b. My son plays the cello really (good/well).
    _____
    _____

21. Put commas in when required.

    a. This diligent resourceful energetic student for some reason is now getting all Cs.

    b. We drove down a rough winding road.

    c. She is a kind generous caring employee.

    d. I'm tired of hearing your mindless hackneyed complaints about this country.

22. What are your memory sentences for the following grammar pieces?

Prepositional phrases
_____
_____

# MICKEY MOUSE, SEMI-COLONS, AND END GAME MUSIC

Past participipal phrases
_____
_____

Present participial phrases
_____
_____

Gerund phrases
_____
_____

Appositive phrases
_____
_____

Infinitive phrases
_____
_____

23. Put commas in the following sentences and identify the significant phrases in the sentence. ("Significant" means it causes a comma rule to apply.)

   a. Writing college essays for my application is not one of my favorite things to do.
   _____

   b. Studying for the biology exam she fell asleep and then fell off the lab chair.
   _____

   c. After the last exam on Tuesday I'm leaving for the Oregon.
   _____

   d. He ran into the room adjusting his Ironman costume.
   _____

# LESSON 5: THE WORLD FAMOUS PROFESSIONAL CLAMDIGGING™ REVIEW — "THE END GAME"

e. On the corner table in your bedroom is your cell phone.

f. Dictating texts with Siri is way better than breaking my thumbs.

g. On the first day of the month we have a 'Soul Music' dance contest.

h. Crying out for help the amateur clamdiggers were submerged under a crashing wave.

i. After the Spanish exam we're going out for some pizza.

j. Feeling the water rise higher and higher the amateur clamdiggers looked about wildly for a means of escape.

k. Dictating to Siri and telling her where to put commas is a piece of cake now.

l. Speaking in front of my peers in class is not at all fun for me.

m. Smiling like a Cheshire Cat she winked at me and took my arm.

24. When do two introductory prepositional phrases NOT require a comma? Give an example.

25. Write out your clause memory sentences for the following grammar pieces:

Adverb clause

## MICKEY MOUSE, SEMI-COLONS, AND END GAME MUSIC

Non-restrictive adjective clause
_____
_____

Restrictive adjective clause
_____
_____

Noun clause
_____
_____

26. What is the difference between a dependent clause and an independent clause? What is an independent clause without a dependent clause? What is a dependent clause without an independent clause? What is a Clamdigger without a clam?
_____
_____
_____
_____

27. Which is correct?

   a. I talked to the admissions person (who/whom) you recommended.

   b. Give this receipt to the guy (who/whom) calls your name.

   c. The driving instructor (who/whom) you met just arrived from New York.

   d. The guy (who/whom) is standing over there by the window, believe it or not, is a Professional Clamdigger.

# LESSON 5: THE WORLD FAMOUS PROFESSIONAL CLAMDIGGING™ REVIEW—"THE END GAME"

28. Now look in the mirror and tell me the truth. **What grammar is still hard for you?**
_____

**Check answers with your favorite teacher!**

---

"Did you answer all those questions? Tell the truth! Kristy—I know you got them. Giovanni, you too? Way to go, G-man. All of them? Felix, you aced it? I knew you would! Are you happy that we are finished—forever? C'mon Felix, where's that famous smile?"

Okay, you're done! First, let me give you a round of applause:

*APPLAUSE APPLAUSE*

Okay, I think I'm ready –

### MICKEY MOUSE, SEMI-COLONS, AND END GAME MUSIC

I HEREBY DECLARE THAT IF YOU GOT FEWER THAN TEN OF THESE QUESTIONS WRONG, YOU

_____
(Your Name Here)

WILL HENCEFORTH AND FOREVERMORE BE KNOWN AS A **PROFESSIONAL CLAMDIGGER™** WITH ALL THE RIGHTS AND PRIVILEGES APPERTAINING TO THIS DISTINCTION. TO RECEIVE YOUR LIFETIME MEMBERSHIP CERTIFICATE INTO THIS SELECT GROUP, SEND JUST ONE HUNDRED DOLLARS TODAY… (just kidding about the certificate, Felix)!

"Thanks for your hard work and your patience, you guys!

"Remember, no more moaning and groaning about gerunds and participial phrases and non-restrictive adjective clauses in public. In fact, you have a responsibility henceforth whenever you hear someone else moan and groan about appositives and the like to get the brothers *to chill out!*

"You can say, for example: Hey **(COMMA)**, man. This isn't that bad! Haven't you ever heard of Mr. Lund's Magical Wheel of Function? Do you play chess **(COMMA)**, by the way? …and so on. You know what I mean? Someone's got to do it, and I must admit I'm not getting any younger. In fact, I think I'm going to go take a nap.

"Oh, one last thing: **YOU BREATHE ONE WORD TO NEXT YEAR'S AMATEUR CLAMDIGGING CLASS ABOUT THE WATERTIGHT, SCIENTIFIC DEFINITION OF A SENTENCE AND NOT ONLY WILL YOU LOSE YOUR LIFETIME PROFESSIONAL CLAMDIGGING™ STATUS BUT YOU MAY BE TRANSFERRED INTO THAT CLASS.**

## LESSON 5: THE WORLD FAMOUS PROFESSIONAL CLAMDIGGING™ REVIEW — "THE END GAME"

"Vee haff our vays of finding out zees sings, heh, heh. Got it?"

"Thanks for flying **Clamdiggidy Air Lund's First Class!**"

**PLEASE CUE THE GOODBYE MUSIC** on YouTube now!—**Louis Armstrong— "Sunny Side of the Street"** This is the official "End Game" music.

"Bye Felix, bye Giovanni, bye Kristy, bye all you Professional Clamdiggers! I love you all! See you in the next book! Keep that groove movin,' Louie! Yeah! I'm stepping out of here!"

**HAPPY CLAMDIGGING, EVERYBODY!**

**Mr. Lund**
**Dallas 2013**
lovinggrammar.com

# Appendix

Memory Sentences for Phrases and Commas
(In the order as presented in the book)

**Prepositional Phrases** (page 138)
In my room under my bed, you'll find my geometry textbook.
 (A partial list of prepositions is on page 133)

**Past Participial Phrases** (page 150)
Insulted by the tone of his voice, she hit the end button on the phone.

(Past participial maker is on page 157)
 She has _____ a lot.
        (studied, fallen, run, etc.)

**Present Participial Phrases** (page 150)
Smiling like a Cheshire Cat, she slammed the door in his face.

**Gerund Phrases** (page 168)
Running across LBJ* is not a smart idea.
     (*a very busy expressway/tollway in Dallas)

**Appositive Phrases** (page 172)
Mr. Lund, my Clamdigging teacher, comes from Chicago.

**Infinitive Phrases** (page 179)
To punctuate correctly, you need to know a little grammar.

# APPENDIX

## Memory Sentences for Clauses and Commas

**Adverb Clauses** (page 201)
Whenever I see an adverb clause at the beginning of a sentence, I put a comma right after it.

**Restrictive Adjective Clauses** (page 234)
Never buy a car that has over 200,000 miles on it.

**Non-restrictive Adjective Clauses** (page 235)
My truck, which is a Nissan, has over 60,000 miles on it.

**Noun Clauses** (page 251)
What you see is what you get.

---

**Memory Sentence for Coordinate Adjectives with Commas** (page 117)
She is my warm, witty wife. (Tip: reverse adjectives or put 'and' between them to see if you need a comma between them)

**Memory Sentences for the Semi-colon** (page 293)

**With a Semi-colon Word** (page 293)
I am a pretty good essay writer; however, I always have trouble getting started.

**Between Independent Clauses** (page 295)
Tomorrow is the big game; we have to win it!

APPENDIX

## Other Useful Grammar

**Linking Verbs** (page 29)

| | |
|---|---|
| I. | be (all forms: am, is, are, was, were, been, being) |
| II. | appear |
| | seem |
| III. | look |
| | smell |
| | sound |
| | taste |
| | feel |
| IV. | stay |
| | remain |
| V. | grow |
| | become |
| | get |

## APPENDIX

**Use linking verbs with adjectives and use adverbs to modify action verbs.**

**LV Adj**
I feel good.
I feel bad.

**AcV   ADV**
I play piano well.
I play soccer badly.

---

### "Strange but Singular" Pronouns (page 60)

1. **Each** of the students
2. **One** of the students
3. **Either** of the students
4. **Neither** of the students
5. **Everyone**
6. **EverybodyAnyone**
7. **Anybody**
8. **Someone**
9. **Somebody**
10. **No One**
11. **Nobody**

(seem/seems) happy.

---

### The Noun Test (page 18)

(The) _____ look(s) great.

Example: **Sammy** looks great.
         The **cars** look great.
**Sammy** and **cars** are nouns.

# APPENDIX

## The Action Verb Test (page 18)

I (or it) _____ (it) everyday.

Example: I **fix** it everyday.
　　　　　It **curls** everyday.
**Fix** and **curls** are Action verbs

## The Linking Verb Test (page 29)

It _____ good everyday.

Example: It **smells** good everyday.
　　　　　It **feels** good everyday.
**Smells** and **feels** is a linking verb

## The Adjective Test (page 19)

It is very _____.

Example: It is very **absurd.**
　　　　　It is very **easy.**

**Absurd** and **easy** are adjectives.

## Pronouns: Subject and Object Forms (page 145)

**Joe and I** are working late tonight. (subject part of sentence)

He gave the late shift to **Joe and me.** (object part of sentence)

Nobody's working tonight with **Joe and me.** (object of prepositional phrase)

# Acknowledgements

Thanks to Jill Pickett, who first helped me to put these "fast and loose" grammar lessons into a polished, uniform format;

To my colleagues at Dallas Lutheran: Tom Couser, Melissa Rankin, Tim Schermbeck, and Kay Meyer, who taught Clamdigging at various times and gave me valuable feedback about the book;

To Mindy Walz, who proofed an earlier version of this book and gave me many helpful suggestions about the manuscript;

To Benjamim Durham, who created the terrific art work for the cover and the book interior;

To Christiana Sherrill, proofreader extraordinaire;

To Anthony Piccolo, Jackie Smith, Sharon Lund, Marcel Lund and Christopher Lund, who helped me with their prodigious marketing expertise.

To Gerry Kosinski, "Wish you were here."

To my father, Willard Lund, and my late dear friend, Ed Trapp, Jr., for encouragement to the hilt.

To Kelly, my wife, for her unfailingly excellent advice and her amazing love and support.

# Bibliography

Warriner, John E. and Griffith, Francis. *English Grammar and Composition.* New York: Harcourt Brace Jovanovich, Publishers, 1977.

# Index

Action verb   18, 32-33, 74
Action verb test memory sentence   18
Adjective   12, 14, 17-25, 73-93
   comma with coordinate   117
   coordinate or multiple   117-123
   choosing versus adverb mastery rule   102
   function   76, 79
   'move'   14, 73-93
   position in sentences   104
   questions   79-80, 90
   test memory sentence   19
   why do we need?   84-87
Adjective Clause   215-245
   causing fragment   282
   non-restrictive   232-238
     mastery rule   236
     memory sentence   235
   restrictive   232-238
     mastery rule   236
     memory sentence   234
   tip with proper noun   239
   tip with 'the'   237
   words   215-216, 230-231
Adjective vs. Adverb (choosing the correct form)   98-106

# INDEX

Adverb   14, 91-97
   examples   94
   'move'   14, 91-97
   questions   95

Adverb clause   194-214
   causing fragment   282
   compared to prepositional phrase   196
   memory sentence   201
   questions   203
   sentence completeness mastery rule   209
   words   195

Amateur clamdigger   2-4
   defined   4

Appositive Phrase   171-177
   mastery rule   176
   memory sentence   172

Brown, James (The 'Godfather of Soul' music)   107-111

Clause   193-261
   clause, adjective   *See Adjective clause*
   clause, adverb   *See Adverb clause*
   clause, dependent   *See Dependent clause*

Clause, independent   *See Independent clause*

Clause, noun   *See Noun clause*

Clamdigger, amateur   *See Amateur clamdigger*

Clamdigger, professional   *See Professional Clamdigger*

Clamdigging playlist   *See YouTube*

Clamdigging, professional   *See Professional Clamdigging*™

Clamdigging sentence   2, 301-304
   punctuated   302-304

# INDEX

Collective Noun   63-69
   list   63
   mastery rule   64
   memory sentence   64
Coordinate adjective   *See Adjective, coordinate*
Comma
   interrupter   270-277, 300
   introducer   265-267
   to change reality   239-243
   with adjective clause   234-235
      restrictive   234
      non-restrictive   235
   with adverb clause   201
   with appositive   172-176
   with coordinate adjective   117-124
   with infinitive   179
   with participial phrase   150-151
      past   150-151
      present   150-151
   with prepositional phrase   137-139
Comma splice   286-289

Dangling modifier   153-155
   avoiding   153-155
direct object (DO)   36-39
   tip for finding   36
   versus prepositional phrase   38-39
Dependent clause   208-212, 281
   causing sentence fragment   208-212

# INDEX

Gerund phrase   161-170
   mastery rule   167
   memory sentence   168
   tip for finding   162-167
*Good/well*   107-110, 112-113
   exception, *well* as adjective   114

Helping verbs   47-51
   list   50
   memory sentences   48, 66
   when checking subject-verb agreement   66-67
   when looking for main verb   48-49

Independent clause   208-218, 281, 287, 300
Indirect object (IO)   36-39
   tip for finding   36
Infinitive phrase   178-182
   mastery rule   179
   memory rule   179
Introducer comma rule   264-269
   mastery rule   266
   memory sentence   267
   Mickey Mouse ('noise') word list   266-269
Interrupter comma   270-277, 300
   list   271
   mastery rule   274
   memory sentence   274

Linking verb   26-30
   list   29-30, 74
   test   40-42

# INDEX

Magical Wheel of Function   14
Mastery and memorization for Clamdiggers, importance of   171-172, 199
Music   See *YouTube*

Non-restrictive adjective clause   See *Adjective clause, non-restrictive*
Noun   14, 18
    collective   See *Collective noun*
    'moves'   14
    position in a sentence   247-248
    test memory sentence   18
Noun clauses   246-255
    mastery rule   248
    memory sentence   251
    positions in a sentence   248
    test   250
    words   249

Objects   See *Direct objects and indirect objects*

Participial phrases   147-160
    past participial mastery rule   151
    past participial memory sentence   150
    present participial mastery rule   151
    present participial memory sentence   150
Participles   156-158
    generating past participles   157
    generating present participles   157
Phrases   128-192
    appositive   See *Appositive phrase*
    defined   130
    fragment   283

    tips for punctuating   181-182
    gerund   See *Gerund phrase*
    infinitive   See *Infinitive phrase*
    participial   See *Participial phrase*
    prepositional   See *Prepositional phrases*

Prepositional phrase   34, 131, 133, 135-136
    eliminating to check subject-verb agreement   54-58
    functions   135
    identifying as adjective or adverb   136
    mastery comma rule   138
    memory sentence   138
    parts   131
    questions   136
    compared to adverb clause   196
    compared to indirect object   38-39

Prepositions   34, 131, 133, 135-136
    list   133

Professional clamdigger   2-4
    defined   4

Professional Clamdigging™   2-4

Professional Clamdigging playlist   See *YouTube*

Pronoun   59-63, 142-146
    relative clause pronoun   See *Adjective clause words*
    subject and object forms   142-146
        mastery rule   145
        memory sentence   145
    "Strange but Singular"   See *"Strange but Singular" Pronouns*

Relative clause   See *Adjective clause*
Relative clause pronoun   See *Adjective clause words*
Restrictive adjective clause   See *Adjective clause, restrictive*

# INDEX

Run-ons   286-287

Semi-colon   281, 291-304
   mastery rule   293
   memory sentence   293
   words   292
      with commas   298
Sentence   4-8
   watertight definition   6-8
Sentence fragment   206-214, 282-286
Sentence, Type I   See *Type I sentence*
Sentence, Type II   See *Type II sentence*
"Strange but Singular" Pronouns   59-63
   list   60
Standard written English   vii, 61, 105, 230-231
Subject-verb agreement   52-69
   mastery rule   53
   eliminating prepositional phrases to check   55
   with collective nouns   63-65
   with "Strange but Singular" pronouns   59-63

Type I sentence   7, 26-31, 40-50
   mastery rule   7
   memory sentence   7
Type II sentence   8, 32-50
   mastery rule   8
   memory sentence   8

Verb, action   See *Action verb*
Verb, linking   See *Linking verb*
Verbs that can be linking or action   40-43

# INDEX

Verbs, helping   See *Helping verbs*
Verb 'move'   14

*Well*   See *Good/well*
*Who/whom* problem   220-231

YouTube
    "Hold on, I'm coming," Sam & Dave; The Blues Brothers   276
    "I feel good," James Brown   108, 185
    "Soul Man," Sam & Dave   304
    "Staying Alive," Bee Gees   245
    "Sunny Side of the Street," Louis Armstrong   315

CPSIA information can be obtained
at www.ICGtesting.com
Printed in the USA
JSHW020351170820
7287JS00001B/2